In her latest book, Diary of a Port Chaplain—My Journey of Faith with Seafarers, *Karen Parsons employs analogies to six pears to describe her 29 years of ministry as a port chaplain among the world's seafarers. The six pears are treats from her life illustrating key aspects of her calling: respect, dignity, love, peace, serenity, and humility.*

Pears are very interesting fruits. When they are properly matured, pears are among the sweetest and most succulent of all fruits. However, if pears mature only on the tree, they become mealy and unpalatable. It is only after pears are allowed to mature off the branches, having been nurtured on the tree, do they reach their full potential.

Diary of a Port Chaplain tells the stories of a person of faith, who, like a pear herself, has been nurtured in the Church but has developed her full potential by maturing her faith beyond the walls of the church into the world of seafarers.

Douglas B. Stevenson, esq.

Director of the Center for Seafarers Rights, SCI NY/NJ

Ships appear on the horizon, enter port to load and discharge cargo, and leave port and pass over the horizon again, in as few as twelve hours. Most persons have little or no contact with men and women who operate the ships and what their jobs entail. They have a much clearer picture of those who fly planes, drive trucks, or operate trains. Few people realize that ships and seafarers bring us such things as Nike products, Volvo cars, SONY TVs, and crude oil for refining into a host of products, and take away products such as American grain, medical equipment, semiconductor parts, and plastic materials for distribution worldwide. Karen Parsons writes lovingly about seafarers as people whose job, in many cases, promotes loneliness, desperation, and a sense of having been abandoned. She weaves her own spiritual journey and the lives and spiritual journeys of seafarers she has met as a port chaplain into a book that should be read in small bites. It is rich and wonderful food.

William T. McMullen, Ph.D., †
Master Mariner

Karen Parsons, the port chaplain at the Galveston Seafarers Center, is one of the few people who have taken the time to listen to the forgotten seafarers who carry goods around the world. Many of these seafarers are poorly paid and spend years at sea, away from their families. Karen has heard their voices and tells their stories in her new book. She tells those stories well. They are about unusual and interesting people-but also about respect, dignity, love, peace, serenity, and humility.

Heber Taylor
Editor of the Daily News, Galveston

Diary of a Port Chaplain

Diary of a Port Chaplain

My Journey of Faith with Seafarers

Karen M. Parsons OFS

NAMMA
New York

Copyright 2014 by Karen M. Parsons

Print ISBN:978-0-9905823-1-1

Ebook ISBN:978-0-9905823-0-4

Published by

The North American Maritime Ministry Association

www.namma.org

To

My husband, Ed, my children and all those whom I love.

Contents

	Preface	xi
	Introduction	1
1.	First Pear - Respect	9
2.	Second Pear - Dignity	40
3.	Third Pear - Love	79
4.	Fourth Pear - Peace	133
5.	Fifth Pear - Serenity	172
6.	Sixth Pear - Humility	204
	About the Author	235
	About the Publisher	236

Preface

A Church which "goes forth" is a Church whose doors are open. Going out to others in order to reach the fringes of humanity does not mean rushing out aimlessly into the world. Often it is better simply to slow down, to put aside our eagerness in order to see and listen to others, to stop rushing from one thing to another and to remain with someone who has faltered along the way.
- Message of Pope Francis for World Mission Day, 2013.

Karen Parsons, the port chaplain of Galveston for more than 22 years has climbed gangways of all kinds of ships and greeted a countless number of crew members at the Galveston Seafarers Center. She has been the steady and comforting presence of a Church which *"goes forth"* in the docks with the doors of her heart always open to welcome seafarers of any nationality. Karen, with her dedicated service reaches out to the load of humanity that comes together with the cargo of the ships docking at the port. In the midst of a fast turnaround of vessels and limited time in port, she is always available to slow down, to see and listen to the seafarers. They tell their personal stories together with the one of their families, they share their worries and dreams for the future, for them she is a mother, a sister but also a friend, a confidant, to whom they open their hearts and in exchange they receive advice, encouragement, support, and prayers.

Now, Karen has compiled all these stories and the letters that have exchanged through the years into a book. While reading it, we have a unique opportunity to discover how these seafarers are not strangers and "invisible" people when they visit the ports of our cities, but they are real and ordinary people like each one of us with a job, a family, with feelings and emotions, even if the color of their skin is different, their names are unusual and they pray God with another name.

Reading the book, we become aware of how many sacrifices the global work force of 1,500,000 seafarers is obliged to do in order to deliver most of the goods that make our life more comfortable. For them the sea and the sky are constant companions like homesickness and loneliness; for months the limited space of the vessel is their home and not always the other members of the crew are the friends that they want and for their loved ones often they are only a voice on the phone.

Though, offering hospitality to strangers and promoting the rights of workers have been the constant teaching and practice of the Catholic Church, through their stories, we realize the importance of the ministry done by Mrs. Parsons and all the other Apostleship of the Sea (AOS) chaplains and volunteers around the world who everyday are enlarging the border of the Church to include the seas and oceans.

PREFACE

Karen is not new on writing about seafarers, having already published two books on the subject: *An Unconditional Love Story; Meeting the People of the Sea* (Mall, 1997) and *I am Your Song; My Journey of Faith* (Mall, 2002). This volume comes after a long time when the original manuscript considered lost, was found intact, months later following the destruction of the Seafarers Center in Galveston brought by Hurricane Ike (September 2008).

What is recounted in the book, however, does not lose its relevance and freshness because all are similar but always different stories of seafarers sailing from one country to another, the dangers of being at sea, the aspirations and dreams but also the frustrations and failures of this people. By telling the stories of ordinary seafarers Mrs. Parsons will lead the reader through the different chapters illustrating the virtues of respect, dignity, love, peace, serenity, and humility, that are universal and recognized by all cultures as basic qualities necessary for our well-being and happiness. Virtues that are a beacon of light and hope for the life of all the seafarers who have encountered Karen even only once.

I am grateful to Mrs. Parsons. With her publication she is paying tribute to the world's seafarers for their unique contribution to society and in recognition of the risks they shoulder in the execution of their duties in an often hostile environment.

+ Antonio Maria Cardinal Veglio
President of the Pontifical Council
For the Pastoral Care of Migrant and Itinerant People

PREFACE

Introduction

THE SIX PEARS

As I quietly sit and contemplate on a beautiful December evening just what it is that my Lord is asking me to do, I feel peace. I long for peace and when it finally comes I am grateful.

For a long time this book has been in my heart. It seems a whole lifetime has passed since my last book. Now it is time to write again. In prayer I ask, "What do You need me to share with them, Lord?"

It was in 1997 when I first met Padre Sergio Durigon CS, a Scalabrini priest from Brazil. He was the port chaplain in Capetown, South Africa when we both attended the Apostleship of the Sea (AOS) World Congress in Davao, Philippines. Then again in 1999, we met again at the International Christian Maritime Association (ICMA) World Conference in the Durban, South Africa. It was there that he became my spiritual brother.

We exchanged letters between our meeting in South

INTRODUCTION

Africa and the next AOS World Congress in Rio de Janeiro in 2002. It was a happy reunion in Rio because we shared ministry stories and spiritual encouragement.

One evening after the Congress session, Padre Sergio wanted to talk to me. He confided in me a deep spiritual matter, releasing all the pain he was holding within. My nurturing instincts kicked in as I just let him cry. It became a major turning point in his life. I encouraged him to find a spiritual director to start working on these things. Soon after our meeting in Rio, Padre Sergio finished his assignment in Capetown and went to Rome for studies.

In March 2004, I had the blessing of returning to Rome where I had been twice before. Padre Sergio invited me to stay at the Scalabrini House, a home for many while studying in Rome.

Padre Sergio, knowing my deep connection with Padre Pio, a twentieth century saint, made arrangements to take me to San Giovanni Rotondo to visit Padre Pio's tomb while I was in Italy.

It is in San Giovanni Rotondo where the story of the *Six Pears* takes place.

INTRODUCTION

Padre Sergio and Me

Padre Sergio and I left the Scalabrini House that day at 4:30 a.m. We walked to the bus stop to catch a city bus to the main bus terminal for an early bus ride to San Giovanni Rotondo. It took us about four and a half hours to ride across Italy and into the mountains. After a little rest and our morning prayers, we were ready for a wonderful day. I was very excited to be going to visit Padre Pio's earthly home.

We arrived in San Giovanni Rotondo about 10:30 a.m. and made our way up to the church. Padre Sergio led me down below the church to Padre Pio's tomb. My heart was pounding in my chest.

The tomb was surrounded by an iron fence with wooden kneelers. The kneelers were slightly angled. That made it difficult to stay on the knees very long. Hundreds of people were waiting to kneel there. I knelt on the floor behind the people on the kneeler.

An old woman in front of me was attempting to say the

INTRODUCTION

Rosary. She kept sliding back on the kneeler. I gently placed my hand on the small of her back and helped her balance until she finished praying. Afterwards I helped her up. She thanked me in Italian.

Suddenly there was no one in front of me and I realized I was so near to Padre's body. I was overwhelmed with humility. Still on my knees on the floor, I bent forward and placed my head on the floor and began to sob. Padre Sergio was nearby praying. He allowed me to pour myself out and then gently knelt next to me and asked if I was okay. After a while he said it was nearly time for Mass and we needed to go upstairs.

We returned to the church and I made my way to find a place in a pew. Padre Sergio went to the sacristy to get ready to concelebrate the Mass with other priests. It wasn't long before he came out to me and whispered, "Follow me." He explained he gained special permission for us to have a private Mass in Padre's chapel. A man led us out the door, through a small courtyard, and into the chapel. He set up the altar for us and left.

Padre Sergio began the Mass. As we prayed in this sacred place, our emotions began to build. I had barely gone through the first reading when my throat tightened as I held back tears of joy. The beauty of the Scriptures overwhelmed us. As Padre Sergio read the Gospel he broke down and couldn't get the words out. I went over to him as we finished reading the Gospel in tears together. For a long time we sat in silence letting the words of the Scriptures surround us, embracing our hearts.

We continued with the Mass. During the Eucharistic prayer we became keenly surrounded with the Presence of Jesus. It was an incredible experience. The Mass took over an hour to complete. By the end we were emotionally exhausted. Leaving the chapel in silence, we walked across the courtyard and back into the sacristy to replace Padre Sergio's vestments. We left the church through a side door.

It was noon and Padre Sergio asked if I was hungry. Yes, I said. He told me he had lunch in his backpack. So there at the side of the church, we sat on the ground for our meal. Padre Sergio opened his backpack and pulled out two bottles of water, a bag and a knife.

He opened the bag and pulled out a pear. With his knife, he cut off a piece of the pear and gave it to me. It tasted wonderfully sweet and juicy! He cut off another piece for himself and then another piece for me. This continued until the pear was gone. All the while he spoke about *respect*.

Then he reached back into the bag and pulled out another pear. Again he cut pieces for each of us and this time he spoke about *dignity*.

Pear after pear came out of that bag and with each refreshing bite came another lesson. All in all there were six pears representing lessons in *respect, dignity, love, peace, serenity, and humility*. It was a wonderful lunch and a beautiful lesson.

After eating the six pears and drinking a lot of the water, Padre Sergio and I made our way up into the hills behind the church to walk around and pray the Stations of the Cross. Station after station we walked along with Jesus. Feeling His pain filled us once again with great spiritual emotion. The lesson of the pears weaved its way along with us.

Hours passed when we realized that we needed to get our return bus tickets. The last bus for Rome was to leave at 5:30 p.m. When we arrived at the bus station 4:30 p.m. we were alarmed to find out the ticket agent was in the village down the mountainside. We had sixty minutes to run down to the village and back up to the station and this is what we did.

As we neared the top again we saw the bus at the station. It was about to leave as we ran up to the door and presented our tickets. Out of breath, we settled into our seats for the long ride back to Rome.

Padre Sergio asked me if I was hungry for supper. I told him I didn't think I could eat another pear. He smiled, opened his backpack and pulled out a loaf of homemade bread, some salami, and cheese. He was laughing at the look on my face and my stunned silence. He said, "My dear sister, you didn't think I would not come fully prepared, did you?" It was a fantastic meal on a wonderful day with my special brother, Sergio.

Six Pears: Respect, Dignity, Love, Peace, Serenity, and Humility. These are the treasures you will find in these pages. These are the gifts I share with you. Each moment of each day has the potential of us finding that window where the Spirit dwells.

THE SEAFARERS

As a Polish/Irish girl raised in a Polish immigrant neighborhood of Detroit, Michigan, which is part of the

INTRODUCTION

Great Lakes waterway system, you would think water and ships would be a big part of my life. The truth is, when everyone else was out playing in the water I was perfectly content staying on the beach making sand castles. My Mom's Uncle Cy was a merchant seafarer out of New York and whenever he visited we were thrilled to see him because he brought his trombone with him and would play it for us. I don't ever recall asking him about the ships he worked on though. And Detroit is right across the river from Windsor, Ontario, Canada. Whenever we took a family trip across the bridge I had to sit in the center seat of the car because I not only did not like water but I was scared to death of heights. Crossing a bridge over water was extremely traumatic for me. So how did a Polish/Irish girl from Detroit end up serving in the Apostleship of the Sea ministry for over 29 years? Because God has a sense of humor. When I asked Him, "How can I serve you?" he answered. Over the years I have had to face my fears every day to climb up over 8000 gangways to care for the people I have been called to serve; the seafarers.

Who are these people? They are husbands, fathers, brothers, sons, daughters, sisters, mothers, wives. They are young and not so young. They are from the Philippines, the Ukraine, Indonesia, Poland, Croatia, Chili, Mexico, Brazil, Peru, Russia, China, South Korea, Ghana, Ivory Coast, Egypt, Morocco, France, Spain, United Kingdom, United States, Canada, Bulgaria, Romania, and so many more countries. They are officers and ratings. They are Roman Catholic, Orthodox, Anglican, Reform Church, Evangelicals, Lutheran, Non-Denominational, Muslim, Buddhist, Sikh,

INTRODUCTION

Hindu, Atheist, Agnostic, and more. They are upper middle class, middle class, lower middle class, poor, and more. There are many ways to describe seafarers. The most important way is that they are children of God just like the rest of us.

For many years I have visited ships and listened to the stories of the people of the sea. In that listening and sharing I have found that it is a place in which the Holy Spirit dwells. On the pages that follow I share with you some of the stories of the seafarers I've been blessed to cross paths with in my life. Now I hope their stories will bless you as well.

1

First Pear - Respect

As we sat on the ground outside the Church of Santa Maria della Grazie in San Giovanni Rotondo, Italy, Padre Sergio opened his backpack and took out a bag, a knife, and two bottles of water. He reached into the bag and brought out a beautiful pear. As he sliced a piece of the pear and handed it to me, he began to talk about *respect*. "My dear sister," he began, "to be able to respect a person we must first know the person. In talking with someone we begin to find out their feelings and thoughts. We hear what their needs are and what is important to them. By listening we are willing to give them worth and value as a person. Respecting someone makes them visible to the world. In the same way we only gain respect from others by caring about others without expecting anything in return. Others can only respect you when you, first, respect yourself."

NICO

I was working in the Port of Detroit in 1990 when I met Nico, a Filipino, age twenty-two. It was his first seafaring job. He made a regular monthly run aboard the ship from Spain to Detroit, Michigan.

I brought my children to meet Nico and his shipmates. They bonded well. He came ashore with other seafarers from his ship to play basketball on the church grounds. He taught some game moves to my son, Danny, then nine. They were buddies.

In mid- August, Nico called home and discovered that his mother was taken captive in Kuwait. Like thousands of Filipino overseas workers in the Middle East, she had gone to Kuwait to work. Saddam Hussein's Iraqi forces had just invaded Kuwait and the first Gulf War was on.

He was teary eyed and worried. With no winter gear, he was also concerned about the coming North Atlantic winter that could be very harsh. In his job as a seafarer Nico earned about US$100 a month. He sent 80% of that back home to help the family. Not much was left for him to spend on himself.

Nico was feeling helpless and scared. I knew that he would worry all the way across the ocean. Before the ship left, I gave Nico several letters to read while crossing the Atlantic. I got the ship agent's address in Spain to have a few more waiting for him upon arrival. I told him that we would bring winter clothing and coats to the ship when it returned in September.

Nico's ship left for Spain. In his hand were my letters. Waiting in Spain were more letters. He felt cared for. He knew that he wasn't alone anymore. He knew there were people praying for his mother, too.

Whenever Nico's ship came to Detroit we, the Apostleship of the Sea ministry team, tried to make the crew feel at home. Often we'd have a picnic or go to a park. Once we were able to arrange for them to get a full tour of the Palace of Auburn Hills where the Detroit Pistons play basketball. That year the Pistons were the National Basketball Association (NBA) champs.

The port closed for the winter in December of that year. We would not see any ships until the following April. In January 1991, I received a letter from Nico with good news:

> *Dear Sister,*
>
> *Thank you very much for all the letters that you send to me…I have good news for you. God heard your prayers for the safety of my mother. She's now in the Philippines December 5. She arrived at least there's no any bad or accident happen to her. I thank God for His Glory. My family are now happy.*
>
> *God bless you,*
> *Nico*

Nico has kept in touch over the years. He got married and started a family. We have exchanged photos of our families and remember each others' families in our prayers.

M/V MESITRIA

I went to deliver Christmas boxes to the Greek owned, Greek flagged ship M/V MESITRIA when they were loading grain in Galveston. Making my way into the crew's mess, I found many sad faces. Even seeing the Christmas gifts some tears were welling but not from joy. On board this vessel were seafarers of seven nationalities. The officers were Greek and the rest were Filipino, Indonesian, Mexican, El Salvadoran, Romanian, and Chilean.

The sadness was quickly running through the mess among the Filipinos and Indonesians especially. They were working on twelve month contracts that ran out months ago. There were men on board for fifteen, nineteen, even twenty-five months! They were tired. They longed to see their families. They were afraid of making mistakes on the job because their minds no longer were on work but on going home.

They asked me to distribute the Christmas gifts to the crew, because if I didn't the officers would take all of the gifts themselves as they did the year before in another port. So I handed out the gifts individually. The ship was leaving soon and I didn't have much time to get help. I contacted the U.S. Coast Guard Marine Safety Office. But the port state inspectors were not authorized to get involved with a labor/management dispute. They offered to forward all information to the Department of Labor, which by law, is the agency authorized to handle labor problems. Unfortunately we never saw the Department of Labor act on any cases in our port.

Running out of time, I supplied the crew with two directories. One was the booklet containing a list of Seafarers

Centers all over the world. The other was a booklet containing the list of International Transport Workers Federation (ITF) representatives in ports all over the world. Both are very valuable resources for any seafarer, but especially a seafarer in trouble. Sometimes we just can't get the problem resolved before the ship leaves port. It is never easy to let them go when they need help.

XAVIER

One morning, amid the hustle and bustle of activity on the docks, a man in the middle of it all stepped out of his important role and into the quiet of his office to visit with me. This man, Xavier, was the chief officer on his vessel. Between Coast Guard inspections, taking on provisions, and cargo operations there is little time for the chief officer to sleep let alone go ashore and relax.

The ship's schedule was tight. In a two week time period this ship loaded cargo in Colombia and discharged in Galveston and Tampa. This tri-port schedule was maintained like clockwork. The ship was in constant motion except for the brief time in port. The ship's officers and crew were in constant working mode. The chief officer was under constant stress. And in the few hours of down time reserved for sleep the loneliness and longing for home interrupted and stole away that precious time.

The night before our talk some of the crew of that ship was able to come to the Seafarers Center to relax and enjoy time away from the vessel. We were able to enjoy them being in the Center with us, although we were well aware that there were others on board unable to come ashore because they were still working. The chief officer, the subject of my story, was among those still working.

Our talk that morning was a true and honest reflection of a seafarers' life. The romantic adventure he longed for as a young boy became a reality when his father gave him permission at the age of sixteen to begin sailing. As a cadet the excitement continued. He loved his work and the adventure of sailing. Over the years he worked his way up in the ranks. Even as he made chief officer his spirit of adventure thrived. He had made several good friends within his company, and as each one married he saw a change in them. He remembers teasing them for being homesick. They told him he didn't understand.

Two years prior to our talk, Xavier also married. In those two years he had seen his new bride twice, totaling less than three months. Now he understood what his friends were telling him. Now he, too, felt the deep loneliness and longing for home. Now he understands the true life of a seafarer.

"The people on land have no idea the sufferings that the people who make their living at sea endure. The world's consumers often do not care how the products get to their countries; only that they are there," he told me. "*Sacrifice* is a word that is the mainstay of a seafarers' life. The world economy would not survive without the sacrifice of hundreds of thousands of people who work at sea. The giving up of a normal life within a home community is an age-old misunderstood ideal, but a major part of all of our lives."

Within the confines of this floating prison, seafarers see the same twenty or so faces for six to twelve months or more. Even looking into a mirror becomes an avoided activity. Coming into a port brings them back into society even for just a little while. They go from being living parts of a ship to being living members of our community. By acknowledging them and their sacrifices for what they provide for our community, we give them respect that life at sea can erode away.

CAPTAIN OMAR

The atmosphere aboard the M/V ATON, an Egyptian flagged vessel, was unusually light and even jolly. The relationship between the captain, officers and crew felt like a familial one. During my visit I heard tales of the practical jokes crewmembers played on each other. The captain seemed to be the biggest joker. There was much laughter and it was refreshing to see.

At a quiet moment when the captain and I were left by the others, Captain Omar said, "I lost my baby." At first I didn't respond. We had all just been laughing. He had just told me how he had the second engineer form a rat's tail out of a piece of plastic to trick the chief steward into thinking there were rats in the galley. Now this man, a young man for a captain, was telling me he lost his baby.

I asked him what happened. He realized he had opened the painful subject and wasn't quite ready for it. He only replied, "It was natural." At that point two men came into the room ready for a ride into town. I told the captain I'd be back as soon as I could.

I returned about an hour later and found him in his office. There was a problem he needed to address concerning the ship and he made several phone calls. When he finished I asked him if he was okay. He seemed to know that he needed to talk about his loss so he began.

He has only been married three years. This child was their first. He loves children so much, yet he lost his child only one month after she was born. The pain was obvious. He blamed himself for being an inexperienced parent who did not know signs of trouble. He blamed himself for not taking the baby to the doctor sooner. And shortly after the baby's death, he was called back to sea. The guilt of leaving his wife was deep.

He described his own grieving process...sleepless nights, waking from sleep full of tears, etc. His depression was keeping him down. He explained that his jokes and humor were to keep his sanity. The men on board his ship were friends. They all worked for the same company for seven to eleven years. They were neighbors at home. They understood his grief and helped him get through the hard days.

From Galveston the ATON was heading back to Egypt. The captain would be signing off there to spend several months with his wife to heal and begin again. We spoke about how God is with him and how He will help him get through this most difficult time.

M/V KOOPERATSIYA

On the morning of April 2, 1996, I made routine ship visits and by now you should know that there is no such thing as "routine" visits. While visiting on board the Russian vessel, M/V KOOPERATSIYA, I discovered the crew sailed without provisions from Africa for fourteen days! This is not a story of a bad or bankrupt company but a story of circumstances. They ran low on food when they were in Africa but could not secure provisions due to the poverty stricken area and civil unrest. I asked them what they had been eating and Alexy, one of the group, said, "Soup. Weak soup and bread." I asked what they ate for breakfast that morning. A young seafarer said, "Bread and butter and tea. This is not good for a man to stay strong."

The captain ordered full provisions upon arrival, but the delivery would not come until late that evening. In fact a ship-wide announcement was made at 8:00am that, due to lack of food, the next meal would be delayed until at least 8:00pm. Meanwhile thirty-two people were very hungry.

At that time our Seafarers Center in Galveston still had a restaurant grill operating and when I explained the situation to Ernie Bright, our manager, he told me to go to the ship and invite them to the Center for lunch at no cost to them. Many of the seafarers came to the Center. And as the burgers and fries were being served to them the smiles and sighs were pay enough for us. I delivered burgers and fries to those who had duty on board and all were truly grateful.

That evening as crews from other ships mingled in the Center news got around about us feeding the Russians. A group of Filipino seafarers from a different vessel donated some money to help defray the cost of the meals. They were happy to know that we fed the hungry because at any given time it could be them in some port some day without food.

REY

Sometimes seafarers receive news from home that causes them much concern and forces them to make big decisions. Decisions that involve a lot of thinking and are constantly pressing on one's mind can put anyone working in a highly dangerous job at higher risk for accidents. In this story, we find a seafarer in a dilemma over his wife filing papers to emigrate from the Philippines to Canada. It was her dream, but not his. To complicate matters, they had a four year old daughter to consider. He needed to talk about it. I listened.

His wife sent in the proper paperwork and was expecting to be admitted to Canada by September. It was March. She is a nurse and had secured a position in a Toronto hospital. The seafarer, Rey, was due to sign off the ship in May to go home. The plan was to let his wife go to Toronto in September. Their daughter would stay in the Philippines to be cared for by her grandparents when Rey had to go back on the ship.

Rey was considering taking a year off to stay home with his daughter. He said the child is very close to her mother and this new arrangement would be very traumatic for her. He was going to give his wife a year to try this and then the family must make a decision. Will he and his daughter join his wife in Toronto or will his wife come back to the Philippines?

The major export of the Philippines is labor. Philippine

men and women work all over the world trying to make a better life for their families. Rey's wife's dream was not unusual. It was just difficult. I've been praying for Rey and his family for years. I hope wherever they ended up they are together and happy.

LEZHIK

I have heard life at sea described many ways: difficult, impossible, extremely trying, adventurous, prison-like, etc. But in 1996 when I met Lezhik, a Polish radio officer he caught my attention with his description of life at sea. He said it is "brutal." Brutal is a very distinct word with a very harsh meaning: savage, cruel, inhuman.

This man had sailed for twenty years when I first met him. He looked much older than his true age. He was tired and broken in spirit. I asked him to tell me about the brutality of life at sea. He began to elaborate, first about his family. He had been married just over twenty years- as long as he has been at sea. He has two sons, one nineteen years old and one sixteen years old. Over the past twenty years he had spent fifteen of them at sea. He realized his last trip home that he really didn't know his wife. He was talking with her and looking at her but was thinking, "Who is this woman?"

The children are growing up without a father. His vacation time, three months a year, was spent repairing things around the house and fulfilling other chores and activities on a list prepared by his family during the nine months he was away. The income he provided was vital to the family, especially with the runaway inflation that was taking over Poland. As happy as they are to have him home, they are more anxious to have him back at sea earning his wages. He concluded that family life for a seafarer is brutal.

Back on the ship, the "floating prison" as so many seafarers call it, citizenship is only a word on his passport. Being away from home, away from community, away from society is not a natural process. He likened it to animals locked behind bars in a zoo. By nature and necessity, shipboard life is anything but democratic. Orders are given and followed. Questions may be asked, but may not always be answered. Often seafarers do not even know each other's names; rather, they address each other by job title. They stand watch, eat, sleep, and mind their own business. Lezhik concluded that life at sea in general is brutal.

Lezhik asked me if anyone on land understood their sacrifices and pain. I must say that I've never walked in his shoes, so I do not understand completely, but maybe a little more than most. I promised him someday I would tell his story to help others to understand a little bit more and he thanked me.

SHALOM!

Back in the mid 1990s, we had an Israeli flagged ship calling in Galveston. The M/V SAMSON came in the first time during Hanukkah. I visited the ship and met the seafarers. They were very good people. Some came to the Seafarers Center to call home.

That evening they were going to celebrate the fourth night of Hanukkah, and they invited me to come on board for the lighting of the candles. They didn't have a traditional menorah, but rather a makeshift one. It was beautiful. One of the seafarers made it from some metal they had on board. It was formed in the shape of their ship and had eight candle holders welded to the "deck".

I felt blessed to be part of that special evening with them as they prayed. Two of the seafarers were particularly happy to have me there. They said I represented their wives and daughters who could not be with them. Their names are Boris and Oleg. Both men are originally from Russia and immigrated to Israel with their families.

For many years Oleg, Boris, and I (and our families) have exchanged Christmas and Hanukkah cards with each other. We have a deep respect for each other's faith. The photos of that special Hanukkah night were lost in the hurricane. All of their correspondence was lost in the hurricane as well, but I found a piece of a letter from Boris dated March 15, 1997 that I'd like to share with you. It gives you a little glimpse into his life.

Dear Karen,

Shalom! Today our ship came to Australia. Now I'm sitting in the Seaman's Center writing you. I am again on the SAMSON. I come back from my vacation.

About my family, as you know I come from Russia before 17 years and married here in Israel. I have two daughters, 11 and 9 years old. My wife is working as a medical sister in a big hospital in Haifa. My two daughters are studying in school and also playing

piano. When I'll come to home I believe it will be June. I'll play with my daughter in concert (four hands). Now a few weeks more is coming our Passover and your Easter. God bless us.
    On this I finish.
    Boris

I have many brothers in all shapes and sizes, nationalities and religions. And I consider all of them a great blessing in my life.

CAPTAIN GEORGIOS

On a ship visit to a vessel named EVANGELOS I met the captain, Georgios. He is a Greek man from Patrias. I spent nearly ninety minutes in his office. He is quite an interesting man.

Captain Georgios greeted me when I introduced myself. He seemed anxious to talk to me, but began with polite conversation. He was feeling out my answers to his questions debating whether to tell me something or not. Finally he asked me what I thought about faith in God and religion and what I thought about angels and the devil! Wow! I knew right then something had happened to this man.

As the conversation progressed, Captain Georgios revealed that something quite intense happened to him two years before. It had very much to do with Satan and very much to do with a visit from an angel. As he spoke he was filled with a real and deep faith. I shared with him an experience I had just a few months prior to our conversation that I believed to be an encounter with an angel. He was thrilled to know he wasn't alone. He hadn't shared his story with anyone for fear of being thought a crazy person. He asked that I keep the details of his encounters confidential and so I honor that. My sharing validated to him that his experience was real. He was so very happy that his ship came to our port. For two years he had been searching for someone to tell, and what a blessing for me that he felt I was the one.

M/V IOANNIS M

The IOANNIS M was in Galveston to load grain in early 1997. While they were there I had a few things to trouble shoot for them. The first problem was brought to me by two of the crew: Joel and Victorino. They had wired money home from New Orleans more than 60 days prior. When Joel called home in Galveston, he was shocked to hear the money never got to his wife. Victorino tried to call home but couldn't get through. Both men did not sleep that night. When I visited the ship in the morning, they asked me to help.

I spent the morning at the Western Union office as they traced the money. Finally the news came that Victorino's wife received the money, but Joel's wife had not. Joel was given a refund and was near tears, thanking me for helping.

Joel's wife had delivered their second son in September and desperately needed the money. Luckily three shipmates were signing off and promised to hand carry the money to her in Manila.

The next set of problems came when many crew members had a big question about their contracts and recent pay tickets on which they all found pay deductions. I reviewed the contracts and pay tickets, asked them questions to clarify facts, concluded the deductions were legal and confirmed it through a telephone conversation with an attorney at the Center for Seafarers Rights in New York. Once I understood the reason for the deduction, I explained it to the crew. It was legal, so they understood and accepted it.

The last problem was the easiest to solve. One seafarer needed a roll of film developed. What a breeze! It was my pleasure to help these seafarers and they truly appreciated our aid.

ROMEO

I was on night duty at the Seafarers Center on January 26, 1998. A young Filipino seafarer came into the Center and said, "Hello, sister." I looked up from my work and saw a familiar face. Romeo had been in Galveston two years earlier. It's always a nice surprise to meet seafarers again.

As we began to catch up on the past two years, Romeo related the story of what happened when his ship left Galveston two years ago. Romeo said they had smooth sailing across the Atlantic, but about seven days out of Spain (their destination) he suffered an accident. Romeo had been using a power sander on deck when it slipped and hit his left forearm. He had a deep, gaping wound that required immediate medical attention. The ship, surrounded by only sea and sky, must be an entity in and of itself. It is a seafarers' work place, home, social space, fire department, recreational area, place of worship, and in this case, hospital.

How was Romeo's wound treated in the middle of the ocean? He was given peroxide to clean the wound and then, without anesthesia, the captain sewed it closed. Romeo said it was the most painful experience of his life. He showed me the scar- it was huge!

In Spain he was sent home where he received follow-up medical care. Luckily, the wound never became infected. Romeo was grateful the captain's hands stopped shaking long enough to finish the job. He chuckled as he thought back of how nervous the captain was when he realized he had to sew Romeo's wound closed.

Of course, some injuries or illnesses are too serious for medics aboard the ships to treat, so they try to keep the seafarer comfortable until they reach a port. Finding comfort on a bobbing ship on the sea is not easy, and many times impossible.

Seafarers make great sacrifices keeping the world economy going. We must make a conscious effort to remember them in our prayers.

PIRATES!

When most people hear the word "pirates", immediately what comes to mind is the classic Hollywood image of the skull and cross bones flag and bearded, swashbuckling, peg-legged sailors with parrots and eye patches. Unfortunately, modern day ships still face the danger of pirates, but the modern day pirates are much different. They come quite suddenly alongside ships in coastal waters in speed boats, and climb aboard the vessels wielding automatic weapons. They still rob the ship's safe and the seafarers themselves, and in some cases wound or kill those who resist.

There are certain known pirate territories in the world. Captains receive warnings from authorities in those regions so they may keep a vigilant watch. In 1998, I received a call from a good friend, a German captain aboard a reefer vessel that called into the Port of Galveston every two weeks. I kept in touch with him after the ship changed routes. This time he called from Charleston, South Carolina. We spoke about many things, among them, pirates.

He related an incident that occurred while his ship was anchored off the coast of Guyana in South America. The captain received a warning that pirates were known to attack ships anchored within ten miles of the coast there. He ordered the ship out to fourteen miles. It wasn't long when he spotted a man in a small boat circling his ship. Immediately he ordered the anchor up and the ship moved another ten miles out.

When evening fell, they kept a close watch on the sea. Soon a small boat approached the stern. Watching it closely the captain saw the small boat turn all lights off. Immediately he ordered his ship dark as well. Another small boat approached the bow. The captain ordered the anchor up and engines forward. The bold move by the captain foiled the plans for the pirates and they abandoned the attack. He and his officers discussed the incident and felt it was God helping them make the right decisions protecting them from harm. He was happy to share that story with me and to let me know he felt confident that God was watching over them.

CAPTAIN IVO

The M/V KUPARI came into port and berthed near a cement silo ship named the CREDA. The CREDA was a stationary ship in port for a long time. As I visited Captain Gordan on the CREDA that morning, he asked me if I had been on board the KUPARI yet. I said no. He told me the captain of the KUPARI was his classmate from the maritime academy in Croatia.

I went to visit the KUPARI next and met Captain Ivo. What a joy to meet this man. Both Captains Gordan and Ivo are from Dubrovnic. Captain Ivo was full of opinions and interests. He told me how his chief cook and he grew up in the same neighborhood. They often talked about their boyhood days. They grew up in an apartment complex that once was part of a Jesuit monastery. They were altar boys in St. Ignacious Church. The Catholic sisters who baked the communion wafers for the monastery cut the small circles out of the wafers and save the edge pieces in a box for the boys. When they were good and did all their chores, they were allowed some pieces of the extra wafer. They thought that was very special.

Captain Ivo spoke about the war that ravaged his country over the past ten years or so. He was filled with emotion when describing how terrifying it was being away from his family at sea when Dubrovnik was bombed. Communications were cut and it was weeks before he received news that they were okay.

He described the pain of having a master's license but

having to sail for years as a chief officer because Croatians were not allowed to be captains on Yugoslavian flag vessels even though they were still part of Yugoslavia back then.

Captain Ivo spoke about his family but especially his eighteen year old daughter who is studying art. When he describes her work he glows with pride. It was quite evident that he loves his family very much.

Happily, Captains Gordan and Ivo were able to get together and go out to dinner a couple of times while the KUPARI was in port. Every Sunday I went to the CREDA to pick up the crew members who wanted to attend Mass at St. Patrick Catholic Church. While the KUPARI was in port, Captain Ivo joined us as well. It was a real treat having the KUPARI in port so long.

CAPTAIN PITE

I first told Captain Pite's story in my book, *An Unconditional Love Story: Meeting the People of the Sea* (Mall Publishing, 1999). We have been friends since I met him on his ship when I worked in the port of Detroit, Michigan in 1991. This is a continuation of his story.

Throughout the years that we have been friends, Captain Pite, a Turkish captain, has called, written or emailed whenever there was a problem or crisis on board and he wanted to share it. For example in April of 1996 he wrote in an email:

During our previous voyage we had two crew members sick suffering from malaria. Fitter hospitalized in Walois Bay. They are taking anti malaria tablets. Now we switched to new kind of tablets but side effects are terrible. A sister ship named ADANA making the same run two to three years ago had a Croatian chief officer who died of malaria.

In early October 1999 I received a fax from Captain Pite saying his ship was coming to Houston on October 8 and he would call me. Houston! That isn't far from Galveston. I called the ship agent for his vessel and found out where they'd be discharging and then I called the Houston International Seafarers Center to find out how to get to that dock.

Captain Pite and My Children, Angie, Danny and Anthony

Captain Pite's ship docked late on October 8. Early the next morning I walked into his office on board the vessel to surprise him. His smile was so big! The ship agent was there doing business. Captain Pite had just asked him where he could make a phone call because he wanted to call me as promised. The agent kept my surprise secret because he knew I was coming. The timing was perfect.

Captain Pite spent the next five hours grinning and telling all who entered his office who I was and how I helped him over the years. We had a chance to have a good talk about family and we went to lunch together. I promised to return the next day and bring my children.

On the 10th the children and I returned to visit and Captain Pite was pleased. He called the children each by name, discussing school with them, and made them laugh. He truly enjoyed having "family" visit him on board that day. When it came time to leave he walked us down to the car. He gave us each a hug and as we drove away he looked sad. One of my children said, "Mom, he looks like he's going to cry."

Captain Pite told me the day before that he receives more letters from me than from his own children. And my letters ask him about how he's doing, not when is he sending more money. He thanked me for my letters over the years saying they are what letters from home should be. We are truly family.

I received a phone call from Captain Pite an hour before his ship sailed. He thanked me for my surprise visit and the visit with my children. It meant a great deal to him. It meant a lot to me too. His ship was originally scheduled to sail to Savannah that trip, but at the last minute was re-routed to Houston. God is good!

Nearly a year later a massive earthquake struck Turkey on August 16, 2000. The quake measuring 7.4 on the Richter Scale, caused thousands of buildings to collapse upon people sleeping inside. The cities of Izmit, Istanbul, and surrounding areas suffered monumental damage. Turkish seafarers sailing on ships all over the world received news of the quake over satellite news and telexes. Seafarers missions all over the world, including ours, worked to try and help seafarers gain information about family members in those regions.

I knew Captain Pite's family lived in that region. I went to my files and poured through Captain Pite's folder to try and find a contact number for his family. I knew he was at sea. In my records I found an email address for Captain Pite's son, Ali. I sent a general email just saying, "Are you okay?" I told them we were praying for them and hoped they were safe. About 48 hours later I received the following email from his son, Ali in reply:

Thank you for asking…I'm really sorry for not to reply your email as soon as possible…we are safe here in Istanbul (Kadikoy)…it was unbelievable vibration, at that time I wasn't home (03:02), I was watching TV at one of my friend's house. After the earthquake I called my sister and mother before the cellular lines were locked. I learned they are safe but very scared. One week has passed but we still feel vibrations…It has started to rain here, it will be so difficult for the homeless people.
God bless us all, Ali

The death toll was in the tens of thousands. We kept the Turkish people in our prayers that God would heal their pain. Then in 2003, there were terrorist attacks in Turkey and I was concerned about Captain Pite's family and friends. Again he was at sea. The attacks occurred in his home city. I emailed him on board his current vessel to ask how everyone was at home. I told him I was praying for his family to be safe. He wrote back:

Lucky as far as I know nobody from our site injured or lost during those incidents. We must gather together to find serious solutions in order to fight back with these terrorists. My country suffered too much and our allies were not supporting in this matter even they support the other side. Now it's bounced and they became monsters to be fight against seriously. They are realizing what kind of problems we were facing. I hope that a solution can be found for the peace but nobody wants peace.

Our correspondence continues as does our friendship and prayers for each other and our families.

DIMITRIUS

I didn't know when I boarded the M/V NORTH SEA that I'd find a fellow writer on board, but that's exactly what happened. Chief Officer, Dimitrius, writes articles about life at sea for his newspaper back home in Chios, Greece. As he experiences things he has the talent of writing them down. He tells the stories. People back in his home town read his articles with eagerness.

He writes with passion as well as humor. He once wrote an article about the wives of ship captains who buy expensive cars and houses forget their husbands must live in a small cabin, be away from the family, and tolerate the life, food, and structure of living on a ship while they enjoy the fruits of his labor. The wives read the article in the newspaper and were very angry. The captains, on the other hand, were pleased.

One of the humorous stories he related to his town was when his ship was docked in Haifa, Israel during the Gulf War. Iraq attacked Haifa with SKUD missiles. Everyone was worried the missile heads contained poisonous gas. Their ship had been equipped with gas masks prior to arrival. The emergency plan was that during an air raid the officers would gather in the Captain's office and the crew in the mess. Plastic tarps would be taped up to seal doorways and port holes and all would wear their masks. They were told by authorities that for four hours after an attack they had to stay inside these rooms and breathe through the masks. When they remove the masks, if they smelled anything like mustard or gas they were to remain in the rooms and put the masks back on.

There was an air raid and everyone ran to their designated areas. The masks were put on and the plastic sealed the doors/portholes. All air vents to the outside were closed and only the ship's air system circulated.

SCUD missiles flew overhead and exploded in Haifa. Everyone was scared. The possibility of being hit was real. The possibility of poisonous gas killing them was real. For four hours the officers and crew stayed locked up in each room. The Maldivian crew became a little restless and hungry. Maldives is a small island country near India. Some ventured into the galley and began cooking. Being from that region of the world, they were very liberal in using curry and mustard.

As the food cooked, the aroma wafted through the ship's ventilation system. Soon the officers, who had just removed their masks began smelling a strong smell of mustard. Not knowing the crew was cooking, they naturally thought they were smelling poisonous gas and scrambled to get their masks back on. They remained locked in the Captain's office with their masks on for another four hours! Meanwhile the crew had a great feast in the mess.

Eventually the stevedores returned to the ship to continue cargo operations and found the officers still in their shelter trying not to breathe curry and mustard coming from the galley through the vents. Rather than being angry from being fooled, Dimitrius and the other officers found humor and relief that they were only breathing in the crew's dinner.

Over the next few days Dimitrius and I exchanged many more stories. He liked reading stories in the GANGWAY newsletter I write for the Seafarers Center. I brought him several past issues.

The ship stayed until the morning of July 4th. I was visiting in the mess early and had to go ashore when the pilot arrived at 8:45am. I stayed on the pier until the gangway was lifted and the lines were thrown. The mammoth ship pulled away from the dock and they were underway. From the peak of the bow I could see Dimitrius waving his cap. Then they were gone....

IGOR AND WOJTEK

Sometimes the encounters are very brief but very powerful. On two different ships I met Igor, an officer from the Ukraine and Wojtek, a cadet from Poland. Each meeting was very brief.

Igor was standing at the top of the gangway when I arrived. He was hot, although it was only 8:00am. The summer sun was relentless in Galveston, and he was facing a long watch in the heat.

I asked him where he was from and he said just outside of Odessa. He had just called home and talked with his mother. She worked full time as a clerk for a bank for many years. She spent all day on her feet. Her salary was only the equivalent of US$35 a month.

Igor spoke about wanting her to stop working, but she insisted on helping support the family. If she quit now there would be no pension even though her pension would hardly be any money. Igor was upset that she had to work so hard for so little. "What is a human being worth?" He asked. Then he was called by the captain on his radio and had to go. "Thank you for listening," he said as he walked away.

On another ship the same day, I climbed the gangway to find a very young man in a very clean pair of coveralls. I told him who I was and he asked me to follow him to the captain. He opened a door and we faced a storage closet. "Sorry," he said, in embarrassment. Then he walked to another door. Through the door he led me up to the captain's office where I visited a while.

I went back down to the deck and found my friend again

and asked his name. He said, "Wojtek." I said, "Is this your first ship?" Smiling, and a little red in the face, he said yes. But not only was it his first ship, it was his first day! He just arrived that morning.

Wojtek is from Poland, and so we talked about his beautiful country. He had to continue working but thanked me for visiting him as well as the captain. He said it made him feel important. I smiled and said, "You are important!"

BIG DECISIONS

The shipping industry keeps the world economy going. When ships are moving their company is making money. When ships are idle, money is lost. The pressures on officers to keep the ship moving are tremendous. Often officers tell me that the people in the company offices do not understand or have forgotten what it is like to be on a ship.

That brings me to Captain Tony. I met him when his ship came into Galveston in the late 1990s. He was feeling the stresses of the job then, and he was on a relatively good ship. His following contract, however, found him on a ship that forced him to make a big decision that could have cost him his job. In mid 2000 Captain Tony wrote to me via email:

Good Day, Sister.

I am still here in Sri Lanka where we carried out some smaller repairs. I told my superintendent in the office that conditions are bad, but he don't care so much.

I'm expecting to sail for India next weekend. There we must make repairs for long navigation. Conditions are pretty bad- we found holes on the ship's bottom and just temporary repair with cement! I still did not decide whether to sail or not. I will tell you–send a message before we depart. Pray for us.

Be good and God bless you and your family, Sister Karen.

Captain Tony

He later sent an email and told me he decided not to sail with the ship to India. He said it was too dangerous. Another captain was flown in to take the vessel out. Captain Tony felt bad for all those who felt they had no choice but to stay with the ship. It was a big decision that could have cost him his job at that company but he didn't think it was worth risking his life over.

M/V COAL PRIDE

Pirate attacks on merchant ships continue to happen. As of January 2010, there were about ten merchant vessels and at least 250 seafarers being held by Somali pirates. The area of attack seems to be widening from the Gulf of Aden farther out in to the Indian Ocean.

Some countries are actively patrolling the area with military ships to aid any merchant ship being attacked, but it is a vast area and the security ships cannot be everywhere. So where does that leave the vulnerable merchant and fishing vessel crews?

I went aboard the M/V COAL PRIDE, a bulk carrier flying the Marshall Islands flag. The ship had a full compliment of Filipinos on board as both officers and crew. They were loading grain to carry to Iraq. The first day I visited several seafarers on the deck told me they were worried because they would be passing through the Somali pirate area. Many of the seafarers had no U.S. visas and thus, no shore passes. They wanted to call their families and talk with them.

I brought cell phones out to the ship and they were so happy! I spoke with the captain and asked him if he would like his ship blessed before they left. He and all the people on board said, "Yes!"

M/V Coal Pride leaving Galveston

On the day before they left I took holy water on board and the captain led me around the entire ship to bless each area from bridge to engine room. Then each of the officers and crew wanted an individual blessing. One by one I blessed them and together we prayed for a safe voyage.

On the day of departure I stayed on board with them until the pilot came on board. I promised to pray for their safety as they crossed over to Iraq. And the captain promised to contact me when they arrived safely. The estimated time of arrival was thirty-two days after departure. The thirty-two days came and went and we received no news. Our prayers continued. Finally on Saturday, February 28 (about a week after we were expecting the news), we received a phone call from the captain saying they arrived safely and thanked us for our prayers.

Since the day they sailed from Galveston we have had several other vessels loading grain for Iraq taking the same route through the Somali pirate territory. They too, remain in our prayers.

Padre Sergio and I finished the first pear and sat quietly for a moment to reflect on the lesson. It was a beautiful day and God was with us.

2

Second Pear - Dignity

Padre Sergio reached into the bag and took out a second pear. As he began to slice pieces off for us to share he began to talk about *dignity*. He said, "Every person possesses dignity. We are born with dignity. We are taught that a just society can only exist when it respects the dignity of the human person. My sister, your dignity cannot be taken from you through poverty, age, disability, religious belief, because you are a woman, or due to your race. Our faith requires us to meet the material and spiritual needs of our brothers and sisters. To raise them up when they are down."

GARY

In August of 1992, I met Gary, a commercial fisherman. Gary is American and a Vietnam veteran. He is a certified aircraft mechanic and was stationed aboard a naval aircraft carrier during the war. Gary was sent home from Vietnam when he could no longer tolerate loud noises. He tried to be a diesel mechanic, but it just didn't work out.

Eventually Gary found his way into commercial fishing and made his living that way for many years. The work was extremely difficult but he longed for the peace he found at sea. When I met Gary, though, his most recent employer turned out to be greedy. After they had the fishing boat out in the Gulf, the captain announced he didn't have the proper license and they were illegally fishing. He also told the crew that if the Coast Guard boarded the vessel they'd be on their own.

Gary and his shipmates were not happy. As soon as they docked back in Galveston they signed off choosing unemployment over illegal fishing. Gary came to see me for help when his captain also cheated them out of their full pay and his duffle bag was stolen. He had no money, no food, and his rent was due in a week.

I went with him down to the docks to talk with the captain of his former vessel to try and get his pay. The captain was very unpleasant and made comments about Gary having to get a woman to do his bidding. We stood our ground, though, and eventually the captain threw some money at Gary and told him he didn't want to see him again. I reported the captain and his vessel to the Coast Guard.

The next order of business was to get Gary cleaned up, a hot meal, and some references for him to be able to get a new job on another fishing vessel. Gary went out on the fishing pier and found another job on a different vessel. After his first run with the new vessel Gary stopped by the Seafarers Center to say thank you with a donation for our help.

EDDIE G

When we first came to Galveston there was a group of retired seafarers who came into the Center every morning for coffee. They'd tell their sea stories and reminisce about old times and buddies long gone. Eddie G was one the group.

Eddie grew up Jewish, but, like some seafarers, wandered away from his traditions. He didn't keep any family ties either, so when he retired all he had were the relationships he made among fellow seafarers and his family at the Seafarers Center.

Eddie and Deacon Tom Hunter, my predecessor as port chaplain in Galveston, became friends. Eventually Eddie was interested in learning about Catholicism. He entered the classes known as RCIA, the Rite of Christian Initiation for Adults. Eddie was baptized a few months later.

Nearly every day we saw Eddie at the Center, so when in the spring of 1994 when we didn't see him for several days we became concerned. We began to ask around town if anyone saw him and no one could remember seeing him for several days. We asked his apartment manager to check his room. Sadly the discovery was made that Eddie had died in his sleep.

The attorney who was named as the executor of Eddie's will was not very kind to Eddie after his death. He laid in the morgue for over a month until Deacon Tom went to court and obtained permission for us to bury Eddie. Deacon Tom was the president of our Seafarers Center Board of Directors at the time. He was also Eddie's godfather.

We buried Eddie on a rainy morning. Deacon Tom and I were the only people present. At first I thought it was the saddest funeral I had ever attended, but the more I thought about it, the more I was happy that Eddie had us. It wasn't sad. We loved Eddie and were there for him. The following evening we held a Memorial Service in the Seafarers Center chapel for Eddie. His buddies from the retired seafarers coffee club came as well as volunteers and staff of the Seafarers Center. Many times when retired seafarers have no one else they have us as their family.

JOHN

One day in March of 1993, I was making my usual rounds on the docks when I visited an American flagged ship that was on a regular run to Galveston. The M/V MARINE DUVAL was in port often, but the seafarers from that vessel seldom frequented the Seafarers Center. I always visited the ship and made a few friends on board. Some were not always happy to see me. I remember the time one seafarer, after seeing me walk into the mess, made a grab for his soup bowl and ran out splashing the soup all over the place just to avoid me sitting down near him and saying, "Hi, how's it going?"

This particular day I visited and found that they'd be in several days instead of their usual 12 hour turn around. A seafarer, John, asked if he could visit me later in the Seafarers Center. I said, "Sure!" That evening John came to see me, but he unfortunately had too much to drink prior to arrival. He was rambling on about his wife in New Orleans who was spending all his money and sleeping around while he was at sea. Not being able to communicate well through the alcohol, I asked John to come back when he was sober. I told him I would visit him on board the next morning.

When I got to the ship the next morning I found John's drinking problem was worse than originally suspected. He missed his duty again and, again, his shipmates covered for him. His best friend confided in me John's multitude of problems.

I tried to talk to John that morning. His major concern was how he could sneak more whiskey and gin on board since having alcohol was against the rules. I tried to focus the conversation on his family problems, but the more John talked about his family the more he craved a drink.

John's ship was in port for six days for repairs. I spent countless hours letting him talk, letting him get angry, letting him cry. I contacted a local Alcoholics Anonymous group to get some information to help him with his drinking problem. On the day the ship was to leave I handed John five letters each dated a different day to open and read on that day. Each letter contained words of hope and encouragement, trust, and faith. John signed off the ship in New Orleans. He called me several times to talk out his problems. His wife had left him. He spoke about leaving New Orleans to make a new beginning, but didn't know where to go.

The calls stopped coming and I lost contact with him for a while. When his former ship came into port I visited. John's best friend was still on board and was hoping I had news about John. He lost contact with him as well. All I could do for John at that point was to pray for him.

In April of 1994 I was working in my office when someone stood in the doorway. I looked up and there stood John! He was smiling and looking healthy. He told me he had gotten extremely ill and nearly died about the time we lost contact with him. He tried to call me from a hospital in Houston, but I never received the messages. He was too sick to keep trying. He made it through the crisis and when he was strong enough he began to ship out again. He was on his first ship since suffering his illness. It happened to run from Tampa to Galveston. He would be in Galveston every six days for the next few months. John's ship was only in port 12 hours each trip in but I made sure I visited and we had time to talk. I always made sure he had another letter to read while his ship was underway. It really was wonderful to see him get his life together. After he signed off that ship, I didn't heard from John again until fifteen years later, after Hurricane Ike swept through Galveston. I received a call from him asking if my family was okay. It was a call that warmed my heart because it was a genuine concern. He is still doing okay and still grateful for my prayers.

PAUL

American seafarers do not have fewer problems than foreign seafarers, just different problems. In early 1994 a tanker vessel stopped briefly in Galveston. A call came into the Seafarers Center from Baltimore from Paul, the husband of a galley cook aboard the tanker. He had been a seafarer himself until he suffered an injury which left him disabled. He asked to speak with the chaplain. When I got on the phone with him, he said he talked with his wife (the galley cook on the tanker) the night before and she assured him she sent him a check to pay their outstanding bills. He said he didn't believe her. She had lied to him before about sending money. He was extremely depressed.

Paul couldn't take it much more and decided to ask her for a divorce, but the agony of this decision was so hard on him he began to contemplate suicide. He said since his injury her attitude toward him changed. He could no longer work, so they depended on her salary and his disability check. He felt he would not be able to live on his own. During the course of the conversation I managed to get his phone number and address from him so I could check on him again and I got him to give the phone number of a trusted relative, his mother, to have someone in Baltimore check on him as well. I called his mother and told her what was going on and she asked me to keep her informed, especially if he got more desperate.

Paul asked me to go to the ship to talk with his wife. I knew he'd be upset when I went to the docks and found the ship had gone on to another port. When I called him back that afternoon the conversation was very disturbing. Paul began rambling on about dying. I kept him talking while writing out a note to my assistant, Debbye Kopecky. I asked her to call Paul's mother in Baltimore and tell her to get over to his apartment as soon as possible.

I kept Paul talking on the phone while Debbye made the other call. I was still on the phone with Paul when his mother arrived at his door. When he let her in, she came to the phone and thanked me for saving him. She said he had a bottle of pills on the table by the phone. She promised to get him professional help immediately. After hanging up, I realized how close he was to the edge and I offered my tears in prayer for his recovery.

ROMY

In 1993, our Seafarers Center staff saved the lives of eight Filipino seafarers who were starving to death when their ship was abandoned by its owners in Coatzacoalcos, Mexico. We fed them for six months via a banana ship that had regular runs from Galveston to Coatzacoalcos that year. After many months of working on this case, we finally were able to get them home to their families. (The original story is told in my first book, *An Unconditional Love Story,* Mall Publishing, 1999)

Word spread fast among seafarers that they received help from our Seafarers Center. A fellow Filipino seafarer heard the story and began to write to me. Romy had his own struggles in life that eventually led to a crisis in faith. I corresponded through that time with him and was happy to be there for him.

In October 1995, Romy wrote:

Greetings in the name of the Lord!... I would like to thank you for all your support i.e. praying, spiritual advice, and moral support during my hour of depression in my career as a seaman. When I almost lost my faith in our Almighty because of the trials and I even lost hope to see the light at the end of the tunnel, you were always there to inspire me. Thank you, Ate.

Romy

CAPTAIN IVAN

On a visit to a ship from the former Soviet Georgia in 1995, I had the opportunity to offer a different perspective in an interesting discussion. I was speaking with the captain who was raised Muslim, but now looks to both the Koran and the Bible to give him guidance in life. It was a very unique discussion. Using both the Bible and Koran, this man found justification in his actions.

Eventually the discussion led us to "taking care of widows and the poor." Captain Ivan explained to me the plight of the people in former communist countries. Unemployment is high and in many places the women in the families are economically forced to turn to prostitution to pay their bills. Captain Ivan saw it his duty to take care of these women by "using their services." He felt justified that his money was going to help their poor families.

I proposed the idea that "buying time" with the women doesn't mean he was obliged to "use" them. Paying for an hour of her time and spending that hour giving her the dignity she deserves is much more in line with the Koran and Bible.

Captain Ivan never thought of that as a solution, and was surprised to see a different side. Our talk lasted about two hours. When I began to leave, he stopped me. He gave me a vase and inside the vase he pushed several photos of the women he "helped" in Poland recently. He took the photos to remember them and their problems. He gave the photos to me so I could remember him and our visit. I told Captain Ivan I had nothing to give him in return. He said, "Oh don't worry! I will never forget you!"

Almost a year later, Captain Ivan's ship returned to Galveston. When I boarded his vessel he greeted me like a daughter, running down the deck to embrace me. As we spoke he told me how he reads the Bible differently now. He was so filled with enthusiasm and said, "You are an angel!"

He told me how his ship is now filled with peace and understanding. I explained to him that I am not an angel but found Jesus in him. His peace was that he, too, was discovering Jesus within himself.

As he skillfully sliced up a watermelon with a hunting knife, he spoke about going home. He would be signing off at the next port and he was going to miss coming to Galveston. We talked about his home and family. I gave him a small crucifix I brought home from Russia. On the back of the cross are Russian words meaning, "To save and redeem." He read them and said he understood.

Seafarers like Captain Ivan are special. They help me to keep looking for the Christ in others.

M/V SETIF II

In March of 1996 we were graced with the presence of an Algerian ship in port. We saw this ship in our port only because a series of circumstances caused them to be there.

The M/V SETIF II loaded its cargo in Houston and began

its voyage back to Algeria. One day out, they began taking on sea water in the rudder well. They immediately turned back and received permission to enter Galveston. While the ship was under repair, the chief cook took ill. Later, at the hospital he was diagnosed with tuberculosis.

With the repairs finished, the ship headed for Algeria. The rudder well again filled with sea water and they returned. At that point, the health department went on board to test the rest of the crew for TB. The results showed nine others with a positive reaction, but the ship was not quarantined. The nine were taken for chest x-rays and all were negative for TB.

The seafarers aboard this vessel were very happy and friendly. They were very much filled with life. During my visits the crew became like family. Rader, the electrician gave me a tour of the engine room. He was a joker and told me some tall tales as we wound our way through the machinery. He even took me back to show me the problem with the rudder.

The chief engineer, Mohammad, had me listed in the duty log as "duty officer" on my birthday. He had me contact his engine room crew on the radio that day whenever he needed to communicate with them. Josef, the Radio Officer, played music from Algeria on his cassette player so I could hear it.

The crew was so full of life. Every night they played pool and table tennis at the Seafarers Center. A cadet named Kamel was especially interesting to speak with. He had studied for many years and had just begun his seafaring career. He was a very gentle soul with a great smile.

The tuberculosis scare made all of us nervous. The public

health nurse and hospital doctors assured us that the exposure was not long enough for infection. Several of the seafarers had brothers and sisters who are doctors and they swamped the phones calling Algeria.

The time spent with the crew of the SETIF II was a real renewal of spirit. Shortly after they sailed back to their region of the world many of them signed off to go home. About a month later a package arrived in the mail for me. It was a gift from all of them; a handmade Algerian dress and a note saying "thank you" for making their stay in Galveston less stressful. It was beautiful!

AKMED

A Turkish vessel came into port to load grain. It docked first to have the holds inspected and take on provisions then it was going to anchorage until the grain elevator was free for their cargo loading. My first visit on board had me seeing some familiar faces and so we caught up on family news. One man, Akmed, a 35 year old fitter, I had not met before. He offered a few words to the conversation and then left briefly. He returned with a cup of tea for me. The others eventually went about business. Akmed sat quietly across from me. I asked him about his job. He answered. I asked him about his family. He again became quiet.

A moment later he asked to speak to me privately. Obviously something was wrong. I went with him to a smaller room off the mess room where less people would disturb the conversation. I asked him again about his family. He took out a picture and showed me. He had three children ages ten, seven and five. They were beautiful children! Quietly he said, "My wife divorced me."

He is a Turkish Muslim from the Black Sea region. In his culture divorce is extremely rare and not well accepted by the community. I continued to listen for the next ninety minutes until he had to be on duty. The ship was going to anchor that evening, so I sent a letter for him on board with one of his shipmates who happened to be in the Center that afternoon.

The ship came back in to the grain elevator less than a week later. Akmed came to the Center and we talked some more. The next morning I visited the ship and Akmed and I spoke again. That afternoon he came into the Seafarers Center to call his mother. After his call we went up into the chapel. He talked a lot about God and the need to have God in his life at sea. He felt more at peace than when they first arrived. Later that evening, after Akmed went back to his vessel, I was working in my office at the Center. One of his shipmates came to visit me. The man, also a Turkish Muslim, said, "I saw what you did for my friend. Thank you."

The ship sailed that night. They were heading to China. Akmed was scheduled to sign off and fly home from there. I hope that he was able to take some peace with him going home.

MARK

On a rainy morning of ship visits in Galveston, I found myself enjoying a cup of hot tea in the mess of a bulk ship at the grain elevator. The chief cook, Mark, took time from his busy schedule to stop and visit with me. It turned out he needed someone to listen.

Mark is a 30 year old Filipino seafarer. He was the one who usually listened to problems of those around him. A cup of coffee and a chance to "bend the ear" of the cook is a scene played out on many ships. This one was no exception. But Mark said when he has pressures or problems, nobody wants to hear it. He was supposed to listen to them.

Mark knew someone was on board who would give him a chance to talk. He is the eldest of seven children. His parents were elderly and the younger siblings were Mark's responsibility.

For many years Mark worked putting his brother and sisters through school. Two of his sisters were now married with one child each. His brother is through school and out in the work force.

Mark spent seven years working in a hospital on an international military base in Saudi Arabia. He didn't go home for seven years as his family relied on him for support. He was 21 years old when he went to Saudi Arabia. He was there during the Gulf War in the early 1990s. He was a survivor of a SCUD missile attack that killed twenty Philippine nationals as well as ten Americans and several other nationalities. His memories are clear and vivid. His sacrifices for his family were great.

Mark's youngest sister was 13 years old at the time of our meeting. He was hoping that in five years, when she is in college and the others are finished, he would be able to finally start a life of his own. He was looking forward to finally being able to be "Mark".

He was happy to have the chance to talk about everything he was keeping inside, although, he said he often spoke to God behind the closed door of his cabin. He said, "I know God knows all my problems, but I tell him just so he knows I know He's there."

Mark didn't need anything from me that day, except to be there, to let him talk, and to just listen. For that short time he was able to be the one to give his burden to someone else. I still pray for Mark. I hope he was able to finally be who he was meant to be.

DOMINIC

Dominic is a Croatian seafarer whose ship came to Galveston twice a month throughout most of 1996. Dominic and I had many visits in which he spent telling me about the troubles he and his wife were having at home. Dominic and I continued talking every time his ship came into port.

On Christmas Eve day of that year, I spent the day on board listening and trying to help him understand the meanings of two letters he received: one from his wife and one from his grown daughter. It was overwhelming for him. He was very moved by his daughter's letter. She seemed to understand him and it struck a chord in his soul. The letter from his wife, on the other hand, pierced his heart. The combination of the two on Christmas Eve was more than he could bear.

Dominic was completely humbled that day. This big,

tough, man I had spent many hours listening to and talking with, who often dealt with pain in anger, broke down and cried hard that day. He cried for a long time. It was good for him to let it all out. It was only after that pouring out of pain and love and guilt that he was able to call home and speak with his family for Christmas.

Dominic and I had two more visits before his ship changed routes. Then he called me from Gulfport, Mississippi before going home. He was going home early in February instead of May as scheduled. He was nervous about finally facing his wife. But he said all of our talks and the letters I sent him kept him from jumping into the water and gave him strength to face his problems. No more hiding from them. I was very proud of Dominic. He finally saw what I saw- a man worth saving.

I anxiously waited for news about Dominic's homecoming. Finally a letter arrived dated April 30, 1997. In it Dominic wrote:

19th of February I came home...13th of March I was divorced. From that time I am living in my sister's house. That was my destiny to be home in February. This time I will not write what happened, but shortly after there was another man...Be sure, now I have no house, no future here in Croatia. Certain, I will need your powerful words, but one is sure what I know, all these hard times, I was not alone. I feel you pray for me and that gave me the strongest will to survive. I am not lost. I believe in love and I will find it...God bless you.

I was in my office eighteen months later when the phone rang. I heard a familiar voice say, "Hello, Sister." It was Dominic! I was so happy to hear from him! He told me that when he went home early in February of 1997 he found his wife with another man. He walked out with his suitcase and never returned. He filed for divorce and it was granted. But then he plunged into a deep depression and went to London to live with his sister. He thought that moving somewhere else would help, but once he was in London he became more depressed. He applied for work on ships through a London company but heard nothing for months. Losing his family and his livelihood was too much for him.

While he was in London he decided he would just end his life so he went out onto a bridge over the Thames River. He climbed over the rail and as he went to let go, he said he heard my voice saying, as I said so many times when he was in our port and he asked why I spent time listening to him, "Because you are worth it!" He stood on the other side of the rail for four hours trying to let go and each time he said he could hear my voice say, "Dominic, you are worth it!" He could hear me tell him again and again that he was a good person and that God loved him very much. Eventually he climbed back over the rail.

He applied for another job and was hired. When his ship sailed to Hamilton, Ontario, Canada, Dominic called me. He told me the story of standing on the bridge and thanked me for saving him. He said he felt stronger than he ever has before and that he knew he was going to find happiness again. He said he'd never forget all that I taught him about himself. He called to say, "Thank you!"

I think of Dominic often. Whenever I do I ask my guardian angel to let him know I'm thinking about him. Then I offer a prayer for him.

THE "STATELESS MAN"

It looks like a passport and functions as a passport yet it is not a passport. A Latvian passport is blue and is issued to official Latvian citizens. The other book is red and is issued to seafarers who were born in Russian territory of the former Soviet Union but have lived in Latvia most of their lives.

The red book lists its holder as "a stateless man" because after the fall of the Soviet Union the government of Latvia refused to grant citizenship to anyone living there whose birth certificate lists a place in Russia as their birthplace. And because of their residency in Latvia, they are not recognized as Russian citizens. Thus they are "stateless men or women."

I visited with a Latvian captain in 1997. As our conversation wound its way through the pressures of the job and the frustrations of the paperwork we found ourselves talking about Latvia.

Captain Andrej spoke of Latvia with both love and pain. He had lived in Latvia most of his life. He loved the Baltic region. Yet when the Soviet Union fell in the early 1990s it didn't take long for the place he called home to mark him and so many others as "unwanted."

As he explained the passport situation to me, he showed me the words that cut him deeply: "stateless man". But it wasn't until he turned a few pages and showed me the page reserved for writing "distinguishing marks" (describing scars, birthmarks, and other physical defects) that I truly understood his pain. In this red book of the "stateless man", on the page describing distinguishing marks is written first, "Russian born". His birthplace is considered a scar, a defect, a reason to distinguish him from others. Captain Andrej said quietly, "It is like the star the Jews had to wear in the camps." Then louder he added, "And this is what I have to give to the authorities in each port," tossing the stack of mostly red books onto his desk.

He opened himself up to me that morning. The pain he had held silently for five years flowed out of him. He spoke; I listened.

Anyone who has ever been on the receiving end of prejudice knows and understands, too well, his pain. Anyone who has ever been told they were born the wrong color, the wrong intelligence, the wrong sex, the wrong economic level, and so on, will know this man's pain. According to the Latvian government, this man was born in the wrong place. Of course, in God's eyes none of that is wrong. It is only our weak human eyes that label people allowing hate, fear and prejudice to rule over love, respect, and acceptance.

"When I was a stranger, you welcomed me." – Matthew 25: 35

M/V AKSU

On the morning of January 27, 1998, I visited with Captain Ibraham on the Turkish flagged vessel, M/V AKSU. He had a lot to say about Seafarers Centers and the people who visit his ship from the Centers. He is a Muslim and understood that most of the people who give of their time to visit his crew are Christian. He respected the work that we do and understood the sacrifices we make to be there for seafarers.

Then he began to talk about where their ship was at Christmas. They were navigating in the St. Lawrence Seaway (my old stomping grounds). He spoke about the cold and ice. He said that just before Christmas they received Christmas gifts from the Seafarers Center in Montreal.

Even though all of the men on board were Muslim, they were touched by the thought that someone in the world cared to make them happy. Inside their boxes they found knitted caps, socks and gloves among other surprises. Captain Ibriham said even he looked into his box with wonder and delight and tried to imagine the person who thought about what to put into his box. He said it was a moment of touching humanity again.

The stories we hear from seafarers about their Christmas gifts are pure and filled with hope. And isn't that what Christmas is all about?

M/V CREDA

In December 1998, a new facet of the port fell into place with the arrival of the M/V CREDA. The CREDA docked at pier 28 and for the next three years made that pier its home.

Slightly smaller freighters docked next to the CREDA to off load cement into the holds of the CREDA. The cement was stored in the CREDA not unlike a floating silo, where it was then off loaded into trucks and rail cars via a conveyor belt.

The CREDA was a working vessel with Croatian officers and Filipino crew on board. They had ten month contracts working twelve hours a day, six days a week, except the galley staff. They worked seven days a week.

Originally there were thirty seafarers on board the ship when they arrived. But due to several problems including improper work visas for crew, many were sent home early. They didn't have proper visas for the long stay in port so as their 29 day immigration passes began to expire crew members found themselves being told to pack their bags.

According to their POEA (Philippine Overseas Employment Administration) contract, they were entitled to their wages for the remainder of their contract since the company was at fault, not them. Instead some were offered two months' wages and then told if they took it they'd be blacklisted from the company. Others were dismissed for various reasons such as being blamed for misconduct voiding their contract receiving no compensation.

The crew shrank to half the original size. The remaining crew had to work more hours with more responsibilities. One day on the pier, a Galveston longshoreman was happily telling me about his job saying, "They're paying us for twelve hours today. This is great! I came here at 8am and we'll go to lunch at 10am. Then we'll come back at 2pm and finish up by 5pm! What a job!" Meanwhile the seafarers on CREDA were the ones really working the twelve hours, seven days a week, but with very little pay.

BRANKO

On March 5, 1999, there was a crew change on a bulk ship in our port. Four days later the new Chief Cook, Branko, a seafarer from Croatia, was hit by a car and seriously injured while on shore leave. He was conscious when he was taken to the hospital. The Croatian Captain of another vessel offered to go to the hospital with me to act as an interpreter. By the time we got to the hospital the doctor was just coming in with the results of Branko's x-rays. The news was grim. He had three fractured vertebrae in his lower back. He would have to be in a body brace for at least two months and then physical therapy for up to a year. It was likely he would need a wheel chair for a while.

As the Captain translated the news to Branko, he lay flat on his back staring at the ceiling with tears in his eyes. The doctor said he was scheduled for an MRI later that day and there was a strong possibility he'd be sent home soon. He asked to stay in the hospital as long as possible.

After the doctor left Branko spoke to the captain and asked to speak to a lawyer. He was afraid he'd be sent home without the treatment he needed. An attorney was contacted and said he'd visit Branko the next day.

The next morning I went to the hospital early to visit Branko. He didn't sleep well. He was worried and in much pain. His head had hit the pavement hard. He had several stitches in the back of his head. Having to lie on his back, the back of his head was throbbing.

I sat beside him. He wanted to talk. He spoke English well

enough for me to understand. He wanted to tell his side of the story as he felt no one was listening to him.

Branko said he had a green light. The right lane was blocked by a truck so he slowly walked to see past the truck and a car came out of no where and hit him. According to the police report, the driver said Branko was crossing on a red light. He insisted this was not true.

I went back in the afternoon to check on him. I found him very upset. He kept shouting, "They are going to send me back to the ship!" I thought maybe he had a nightmare, but soon I heard the same news. The trauma nurse, social worker and attorney for the ship owner showed up. The wheels were in motion for Branko's discharge.

The doctor came in and downplayed Branko's vertebrae injury, saying it was not so severe. The doctor also gave him news that he had two fractured ribs. The trauma nurse suggested maybe Branko could stay a couple of weeks in Galveston to begin to heal. The ship owner's attorney said Branko had only two options: to go back to work on the ship or to go home.

Branko protested saying he was in too great of pain to go all the way home on a plane. Just five days before he had travelled thirty-six hours to get here by plane. He just couldn't imagine having to travel that long and that far in such pain. And to go back on board the ship! He couldn't work so what would be the point? The pain he would suffer with the rolling and pitching of the ship as the ship crossed the ocean going to Turkey would be unbearable. Branko's eyes were filled with fear.

Two hours later the attorney obtained for Branko arrived. Being told about the pending discharge he said there was nothing he could do to stop it. None of us– Branko, the trauma nurse or myself– understood why. It was very frustrating.

Branko's ship left Galveston and had gone to Houston to load the cargo for Turkey. The ship owner's attorney's plan was to arrange for Branko to be driven up to the ship in Houston. It was definitely cheaper to put him back on the ship than on a plane home and pay for plane fare for his reliever.

Branko had to use a walker to get from his bed into the lavatory to use the toilet. Every step shot pain up his back. He was perspiring heavily and his arms were strained as he held up his body.

Unbelievably Branko was packed up and driven to Houston to join his ship. He was aided by his shipmates in climbing the gangway and taken to his cabin. I spoke to his captain by phone and the captain said Branko was in too much pain. He couldn't take the responsibility of hurting his back worse on the sea. The ship was due to leave for Turkey that night. The captain convinced Branko he needed to sign off and fly home. The company arranged for Branko to spend that night in a hotel and be put on a plane the next morning.

The buzz on the ships in port reached outrage. Seafarers heard about a fellow seafarer being hit by a car and asked what happened to him. When they were told, no one could believe he was actually taken back to his ship when he couldn't walk and couldn't work. One officer said, "We cannot be sick or injured because we are not human beings in their (the company) eyes. We are replaceable parts of the ship. Pray for us."

M/V THETIS

On January 29, 1999, the M/V THETIS came into port to discharge cement. They arrived with one man missing. A seafarer named Paulus disappeared while the ship made its crossing from Korea to the Panama Canal. Understandably the crew was very upset. The US Coast Guard launched an investigation interviewing officers and crew members. No conclusive evidence or information was shared, although crew members complained of excessive overtime of which they were consistently cheated out of pay, food was being rationed and conditions were bad for living. Many had been sleeping on the deck because of no air conditioning or circulation of air in the cabins; they speculated Paulus fell overboard while sleeping.

The crew called the International Transport Workers Federation (ITF) representative in Houston to help them. He was unable to visit the ship in Galveston, but they were due to sail to Houston for loading after discharging the cement in Galveston. They hoped he would visit them in Houston.

One of the evenings they were still in Galveston, Fr. Page Polk OFM, accompanied me to the vessel to say Mass for Paulus' soul. Afterwards, the two of us spent much time on board counseling the crew. Many were telling us things quietly that they were suffering. When asked if they wanted me to help they said they were afraid.

The ship finished discharging the cement and went to anchor for a week to clean the holds so they could load grain in Houston. The captain ordered two fitters, who normally do not clean holds, to clean them. They worked fifteen hour days for a week, scraping and spraying the cement off the walls of the holds. When it was finished the Captain paid them only US$80 each which was roughly seventy-eight cents an hour.

The THETIS docked in Houston on February 11. I notified the port chaplains in Houston to keep an eye out for them. On the 12th of February I went to Houston to teach at the Houston Port Chaplaincy School. While I was up there I gained permission to visit the THETIS at the Houston berth. They were very surprised to see me. They were losing hope for any relief in the situation on board. The Houston chaplains arranged for the ITF representative to meet with the crew away from the ship that night if they wanted him to help them.

Later that evening only two seafarers from the THETIS came off to meet the ITF representative and so nothing could be done for them. The ship sailed and the voices were silent.

HOSPITAL DUTY

Part of my duties as port chaplain is visiting the hospital when a seafarer is ill or injured. On a day in mid 2000, I visited our hospital and found a seafarer critically injured in a knife attack aboard a cruise ship in the port of Houston. The dynamics aboard a passenger ship are much different than aboard cargo ships.

People from many countries compete daily for jobs, promotions, better schedules, etc. Tensions can run high among crew members especially those non-seafaring crew members such as hotel and wait staff, hospitality, bar tenders, etc.

A young man from the Dominican Republic sailed as the assistant food and beverage manager. On that day, he was making his rounds checking on different departments under his supervision when he was attacked by a Jamaican crew member. He sustained stab wounds to his abdomen, chest, arms, and face. The Jamaican worker had been demoted earlier in the day by the chief food and beverage manager.

The injured man was brought to our hospital in Galveston for surgery and recovery. He would be sent home once he was well enough to travel. The attacker was taken into custody by the authorities.

My visit with the young man in hospital found him awakening from a bad dream. I stayed with him for a long time as he talked about the attack. He was completely surprised by it. He was in pain as he had many repairs done inside and outside his body. His body would eventually heal, but his emotional healing would take much longer.

CAPTAIN JANUSZ

On January 5, 2001, I was still giving out Christmas gifts and ended up on Captain Janusz's ship. His ship was loading for a long voyage to Europe. On board where seventeen seafarers: one Polish, one Croatian, and fifteen Filipinos.

The crew was surprised with the gifts. I explained it was

only the twelfth day of Christmas and since they weren't here with us for the holiday, we were happy to surprise them with gifts now. After settling all the gifts in the mess, I went to greet the captain. I found Captain Janusz in his office. There, too, I found the Chief Engineer, Josef. Janusz is from Poland and Josef is from Croatia.

They invited me to sit with them and have some tea and our conversation began. Both men are Catholic and were curious about me being a Catholic port chaplain. Such roles for Catholic women in Europe did not exist for the most part. Josef went off to gather some things to show me. Soon he was back carrying a five hundred year old icon of St. Joseph that he brings with him on every ship. Another item he had was his prayer book, which appeared to be falling apart. It, too, was hundreds of years old. Inside the prayer book were many holy cards dated 1854, 1810, 1732, and so on. It was very interesting.

When Josef went back to his cabin to replace his special items, Captain Janusz began to talk of the difficulties of life at sea. And then, as if he had sparked something within himself, began to talk about his father.

Janusz's father was a doctor and his four brothers were also doctors. Janusz was supposed to study to be a doctor as well but he didn't pass the exam the first time. He had to be in school to avoid serving in the Russian-backed Polish Army, so he entered the marine academy.

Janusz brought out pictures of his family. His wife and three daughters live in Szczecin, near Germany. His eldest daughter is a doctor. Among his photos was a picture of his father, which caused Janusz to start thinking of him again. He told me his father had a very hard life. He was a doctor and a soldier in World War II. When Germany rolled across Poland's border in September of 1939, Janusz's family would never be the same.

His father was captured by the Germans and forced to march for miles toward an internment camp. They were not given food or water. The POWs were offered water by old women along the road, but the German soldiers killed the women for offering it. The POWs were only allowed to drink the dirty water in the ditches along the way. Many got dysentery and died. Janusz's father was one who became extremely ill, but fortunately survived.

Once at the camp he was forced to work as a doctor to take care of wounded Germans. After he was released, the Russians accused him of aiding the Germans and forced him to work as a doctor in another camp. At that camp was an outbreak of typhoid and Janusz's father again nearly died in the epidemic.

All the while his mother did her best to raise the boys. When the war ended, his father returned and began his private practice but that was short lived. When the Korean War broke out, the military once again came for his father. With a wife and five sons to feed, a military salary did not help much. Janusz's mother began selling pints of her blood to buy them shoes or food or clothes.

Janusz's story was more of a reflection on the harshness of life. It seemed that by telling me the hard realities of his father's life, the hard realities of Janusz's life were bearable again. I was with him nearly two hours that afternoon. His ship sailed that evening. I hope his heart was a little lighter.

JONATHAN

"Hi, Lai, remember me?" Of course I remembered him. He called me "Lai" back then too. Jonathan, a Filipino seafarer, whom I hadn't seen since 1999, was back in port. It was 2003. I asked him how his family was doing. He lowered his eyes. I asked, "Is everything okay?" He said, "After we left here in 1999, I went home to find my wife, Eleanor, diagnosed with terminal cancer." She died just a couple of months after he got home. She was forty-two. He has two daughters whom he had to leave shortly after their mother's death so that he could get back to sea and earn a living to pay for their schooling. They stay with Jonathan's sister-in-law when he is at sea.

I gave Jonathan my condolences and told him I had lost my father six months earlier to cancer as well. He was saddened by this news too. Then he said, "Did you hear the news about our captain?" I said no. He told me that their captain killed himself just outside the port of Boston a few months prior. He was really disturbed by this happening. So we talked about it. It was the first time he talked about it since it happened.

The captain, also a Filipino, was found hanging in his cabin. There was no note but a Coast Guard investigation determined it was a suicide. The speculation was the pressure of the job got to him. He was married with four children. The captain was only in his early forties. The new captain was from Poland.

Jonathan stayed a while at the Seafarers Center that evening. He said they were sailing soon and that they may be back before the end of the year. It was good to see him again. I told him that he and his family would be in my prayers.

M/V CIC PIRAEUS

On November 3, 2003, I boarded the M/V CIC PIRAEUS to greet the crew. That is when I found they had no visas and therefore, no shore passes. They were very upset. Following the attacks of September 11, 2001, tight security restrictions found ships' crews being denied shore access in ports all over the United States.

For several days the CIC PIRAEUS was in port loading grain. I visited often trying to meet their needs the best I could under the circumstances. The Filipino crew requested a Mass to be said on board since they couldn't get to a church on shore. I contacted my parish in Galveston and Fr. John Paul made arrangements to say Mass on November 4.

That evening we gathered in the crew's mess. Captain George, a Greek veteran of the sea, joined us. The service was beautiful. Captain George provided special incense from a monastery in Greece and Fr. John Paul said the Mass for the Dead in commemoration of All Souls Day (November 2).

Following the Mass, Captain George invited us to stay for dinner. It was a lovely evening and we had a good visit with all the crew.

The following day, I delivered Christmas gifts to the ship as they were leaving for a long trip to Israel. On that morning Captain George and I stood out on the deck talking for a long time. He's been at sea over twenty years and this was the first time he was ever denied a shore pass in the United States. He found it extremely insulting as he spoke about how his uncles fought alongside American soldiers in Korea and his grandfather alongside American soldiers in WWII. He spoke about how directly after the attacks on September 11, 2001, the world felt deep sympathy for the U.S. and outrage toward the terrorists for such a cowardly act but how the tide has turned with all that has happened since. The sympathy has gone away and is being replaced by a very negative view of the U.S. overseas. He said it is very sad.

He spoke about how his crew could only complain about not being able to call home. They were afraid to even go down on the pier to check the waterlines for fear of being fined by Immigration for being on land. He said they had no rest, no recreation while they were here. They only felt the continuous vibration of the ship's engines on the steel deck beneath their feet. He said the economy of Galveston lost out on twenty-four people shopping in their stores, eating in their restaurants, spending money in their city. I let him vent. Who else is he going to vent to?

EARLY ONE MORNING

The ship, POLYDINAMOS, was loading grain. It was December 2006. On board was an entire crew of Ukrainian seafarers. Many had no shore passes and so our Seafarers Center provided cell phones on board so they could call home. Sometimes the timing of getting back on board to pick up the cell phones before the ship sails can be tricky.

On the night before they were due to leave I asked what was the estimated time of departure (ETD). I was told I needed to be on board at 6:30am to pick up the phones.

Early the next morning I went to the ship. It was still dark. Everything was quiet. There was one man on watch at the top of the gangway. I explained I was there for the phones and he said, "You are very early." I explained I was told the ship was leaving very early. He called the duty officer, Victor. Again I explained why I was on board so early. Victor said, "No, we are not leaving until late afternoon, but I will call and wake up the 3rd officer who has the phones in his room." I stopped him and said I would be back around noon. He agreed.

As I began to leave Victor said, "Please could you stay and have a cup of tea?" The few days they were here we had been listening to their fears over the turmoil of the Ukraine election. I knew that's what Victor needed to talk about so I went into the mess room and had a cup of tea with him. And as I guessed he began to talk about the dangerous political situation at home.

Victor was very interesting to listen to as he explained the dynamics of what was really happening in this political battle. There was a wall map on which he showed me the regions that were for Yanukovych or for Yushenko. He explained that Russia backed Yanukovych and the U.S. backed Yushenko. And even broke it down further to say it was coming down to Orthodox vs. Roman Catholic.

He talked, I listened. He let his fears flow and I gathered them up. The sun rose and the ship began to come alive with sleepy seafarers wandering into the mess for breakfast. All thanking me for the use of the phones and the Christmas gifts we brought on board.

Victor walked me down to the gangway and said, "They all fear for their families." I promised to pray for them. At the gangway a very young seafarer waited for me and digging in his pocket he pulled out a little "Jolly Rancher" candy and said, "For you!" I thanked him and thanked Victor for the tea and went down the gangway.

M/V NORD LONDON

On November 19, 2013 I received a call from a ship agent informing me of the death of a seafarer. He asked me to meet the launch bringing his body to shore the next morning and pray over him before the medical examiner took him for autopsy. The next day it was raining when the launch arrived. I boarded the launch and was joined by two of the crew on the aft deck. One of them held an umbrella over me as I opened my prayer book and began to read the prayers of the dead. I blessed the body of Solidan Trazo, 36, of the Philippines and he was then taken by the medical examiner for autopsy. The ship was held at anchorage until the autopsy was complete. The cause of death was complication from malaria.

On November 29, 2013 the NORD LONDON, Singapore flag, docked at Texas International Terminals in Galveston. I boarded the vessel at 9:30am prepared to lead a memorial service with the crew. The USCG was on board conducting an inspection. I waited in the mess for the crew to have a chance to come together. Whenever they could one or another would run into the mess and tell me bits of information. Eventually they handed me a list of problems that they all signed. The problems on the list included many things such as not being administered anti-malaria drugs prior to entering known malaria zones, not being paid on board wages in three months, food being rationed (two months provisions stretched to three months), and many more complaints.

Crew of the M/V Nord London

I worked with Doug Stevenson at the Center for Seafarers Rights since this was a MLC 2006 case and Singapore is a signatory state on the treaty. The Coast Guard MSU – Texas City did an outstanding investigation. Lloyd's registry was on board several days as well. My understanding is the investigations resulted in issuance of an ISM (International Safety Management) major non-conformity.

I held the memorial service one evening after the inspectors left for the day. The 3/O was going to read the first reading and when he began to read he stopped and began to cry. The others followed. I finished the readings for them. We had a long talk that night about what they experienced watching their shipmate suffer and die. I also blessed the cabin where the seafarer died and the cabins of all the seafarers. They were very grateful.

Pressure mounted on the captain and he was ordered by the company to respond immediately in writing to answer each of the allegations and provide documentation. I spent approximately 15 hours on board the vessel over 3 days. The captain saw me in the mess working with the seafarers and saw Coast Guard inspectors talking with me from time to time. He didn't greet me when I greeted him.

On Saturday, November 30, 2013 my husband, Ed accompanied me to the vessel as it appeared I would not be spending much time with the family over the Thanksgiving weekend and he was interested in helping the seafarers as well. We brought 20 Christmas gifts to them with much needed toiletries since they could not go shopping for lack of money. We also bought 20 bottles of mosquito repellant with deet so that each person could have their own bottle for their voyage back to Africa. We brought 20 packages of Vanilla Oreo cookies to put in the freezer for the trip over to Africa (the crew's favorite and they had no snacks or desserts in months) and on Friday night after spending seven hours on board with them I came home and baked six dozen oatmeal chocolate chip cookies for immediate consumption when we arrived on Saturday. We also each heard more stories from crew members. They were greatly appreciative of him coming with me and spending the day on board with them.

I let the Coast Guard do their job, the Singapore flag authorities do their job, the Lloyd's registry inspector do his job. The facts were all there. I remained on board for hours for pastoral care of the seafarers. On the last day, once the inspections were all done, I turned my attention to the master. The ship agent told me that the crew would be paid on Monday, December 1. He said the money was on board. I waited until 1600 and still no pay had been distributed. A pilot was ordered for 1930. I went to the captain's office. He looked exhausted. I asked him if I could speak with him. He said he was very busy. I told him I knew he was very busy and I had been very busy with the crew the past few days. But I came to ask him if there was something I could do for him. He said no, but I didn't leave. He sat down and began to talk about all the pressures he has a captain and how the industry has changed. The stress was great and the responsibility was crushing. I listened for 30 minutes. He said he called his wife and told her he can't take it anymore and this is his last trip. He is going to retire when he signs off in Africa. He wanted to sign off in Beaumont but the chief officer is signing off there so he must stay. I asked him if he was from Goa, since his family name was Spanish sounding and he said yes. I asked him if he was Catholic and he said yes. Then I spoke to him about what it means to be Catholic and how we treat people, how we live in this world as someone who follows Christ. I asked him if he had the crew's money on board. He said yes. I told him that I was going to go down to the mess and wait while he called the crew up to pay them. He shook his head. I left his office and as I walked down the stairs to get to the mess I heard the announcement for all hands to come to his office for pay. Seafarers were running past me very excited. In the mess I waited. One by one they came back down with big smiles and said, "Thank you, Mom." We had a talk afterwards about them praying for the captain and to keep in touch with me via email as they cross the Atlantic. They asked me to contact the Beaumont Seafarers Center and ask if anyone there could take them shopping when they get in. They are anxious to buy laptops to communicate with their families. They have internet access on board. They really were happy to have some money to go shopping. That is the only thing they asked me to ask them to do besides to have a Mass on board.

I contacted the Seafarers Center in Beaumont and Fr. Sinclair to alert them to the NORD LONDON heading their way. I sent my report and asked them, for the crew, to please arrange for shopping and a Mass on board when they arrive. I also asked for someone to give the Captain some more pastoral care. He is exhausted and burned out. He just needs someone to listen to him and encourage him.

The USCG did all they could do within the perimeter of their regulations. The audit conducted by Lloyd's registry resulted in a major non-conformity with the ship's safety management system. The Captain must now undergo additional safety management training with his company since anti malaria tablets were incorrectly administered. The auditor from Lloyd's Registry has deemed that the company must update their Safety Management System to include procedures to prevent malaria when entering malaria zones worldwide. I was told that this company has over 20 vessels so this action should help protect over 400 seafarers in their employment.

Another pear was finished. Dignity. Yes, it was time to be quiet and let the lesson find its place in my heart. The pears tasted awfully good and the water was so refreshing!

3

Third Pear - Love

Padre Sergio reached into the bag and brought out the third pear. This one he said is the lesson on *love*.

"God is love, dear sister. Caring for people, that we may only meet once in our entire life as if they were part of our own family, is love; agape love. This is a spiritual love that once someone experiences it, they will never forget it because God is present. Not everyone will understand this love but they will feel it and wonder about it and it will change hearts."

M/V POSYET

Sometimes entire crews capture our hearts, especially when they come on a regular route to our port for several months. From August 1992 to January 1993 I had the wonderful pleasure to get to know the Russian crew of the POSYET. They sailed into our port every Tuesday for four months.

Every Tuesday for four months they were denied shore passes. So every Tuesday for four months I was their English and current events teacher, mail lady, bargain shopper, newspaper delivery person, birthday celebrator, confidant, and friend.

My memories are deep, though the crew has been gone nearly two decades. I still remember Petr's eyes sparkling as he spoke about his children. He struggled to learn English and in each of our English lessons he spoke only of his family making it very clear how important they are to him.

I remember how I explained to them the first time I showed up with a birthday cake with candles for Vladimir's birthday. I showed him how to make a wish and blow out the candles. Then they all were excited about celebrating birthdays. Before the end of October we had birthday parties for Vladimir, Alexsandre, and Mikhail.

So many times I was on board the second officer, Aleksandre, ran past the door of the lounge or mess where I was visiting with others and apologize for being so busy. But one afternoon he had time to visit and he spent an hour talking about home: Vladivostok.

The bosun, Yerman, always stopped in to talk with me whenever I visited. He didn't speak much English, but he told me many stories in Russian. I enjoyed listening to him because he was a great story teller. His expressions and voice changes were wonderful. Later, Alexsey, a cadet, translated the stories into English if I didn't understand parts of them. Alexsey spoke the best English on board. I always brought him a Galveston and Houston newspaper whenever they were in port. He'd translate the important stories to his shipmates at meal time.

Valentina worked as a stewardess in the mess. She assisted Rimma, the chief cook. Valentina always brought me a cup of tea whenever I visited. Her focus in life was her son, his wife and her new granddaughter. She asked me to find some books for children with pictures and easy words so she could teach her granddaughter English. She was so happy when I came to the ship with an armful of the best children's books I could find.

Rimma, a wonderfully jolly woman, also had a request for me. She asked if I would order her some "cowgirl" boots from the Sears catalog. When I agreed she was so tickled she also asked to order a new winter parka. When it arrived and I brought it to the ship, she modeled her new (red) boots and parka for all of us!

After becoming so close, there was a morning when the six youngest members of the crew came and asked me to tell them about AIDS. I asked them what they knew about it themselves and they said they were told there were only five cases of AIDS in all of Russia and it was nothing to worry about. I told them I'd be back with some information and then we'd talk. Later that day I returned with statistics and articles on the AIDS crisis around the world. The young men were shocked to learn the scope of this disease. They had many more questions about many more things after that.

On January 5, 1993 the entire crew of the POSYET had their bags packed and were ready to go to the airport to go home. The new crew was on board. The outgoing crew introduced me to the new and explained how much I helped them. Immediately the man who served as the ship's new doctor asked me to help him update the ship's medicine cabinet with over- the- counter medicines. I left for the store with his list as my friends left for the airport. I knew I would miss them incredibly, but I didn't have time to grieve their departure. It was time to help the new crew. A few weeks later the doctor returned the favor when I asked him for help in explaining the dangers of consuming rubbing alcohol to a Russian crew on a different vessel. To them it was "cheaper than vodka". The doctor's explanation to them in Russian fortunately got the message across, whereas my skull and crossbones drawing on a piece of paper only confused them thinking I was talking about pirates.   The mission continued.

THE LYKES GUYS

Eddie G (from the story in Chapter Two) was part of a group of seafarers we called the "Lykes Guys". They were members of the old National Maritime Union (NMU), which has since merged with the Seafarers International Union (SIU). They all worked on the Lykes Line vessels. Back in the early 1990s, when I first arrived in Galveston, the Lykes Line still had many ships regularly calling into Galveston's port. Many of the seafarers who sailed those vessels came into our Seafarers Center whenever their ship was in port or when they were in town waiting to join their ship, which was due to arrive soon. Many of the Lykes Guys lived in Galveston.

During that time period we also had some retired seafarers in the mornings drinking coffee, talking politics, and reminiscing about their days at sea. The ones I remember most are Eddie G., Pete, Louie, Lester, and Little John. I already told you about Eddie G. except that I failed to mention in his story that he always wore Bermuda shorts, a polyester shirt, and an ascot tie and he liked to slick his hair back with tonic. He was a nice man.

Pete always wore a light blue or yellow cotton shirt and dark pants on his small frame. He was very ornery and always wanted to fix something around the Center. He had strong opinions on many subjects and didn't like when new locals came into the Center. He wanted to make sure they were really seafarers before they were allowed to hang out. He was very protective of the place. Sadly, Pete died of cancer about ten years after I met him.

Louie was older than the others, but he was there every morning as well. He listened more than participated in the conversations but loved being with his friends. When Louie didn't show up one morning, Pete went out looking for him. Louie always walked from his apartment to the Center. Pete found Louie dead on the sidewalk only a few blocks away. It was determined that there was no foul play. He had just died while on his walk to the Center.

Lester was an even shorter guy than Pete. He wore very thick glasses and spoke with a gruff voice. His voice sounded mean, but he was actually very nice. Lester was married and lived locally after his retirement. For many years, Lester had ailments and constantly had doctor's appointments. One day I received a call from his wife, telling me Lester was in the hospital. I went to visit him and found he was dying of throat cancer. He didn't have long. I stayed with him and prayed for him and when he died, helped his widow get a decent burial for him through the Veterans Administration because he served in the Navy for many years prior to his merchant marine service.

That leaves Little John from that group. One day Little John handed me a small photo of himself. That was the day he told me he was dying of cancer and asked me to pray for him. He died just weeks later. I kept his photo in my desk for years. It reminded me of all these guys. That photo was lost in Hurricane Ike along with everything else in my office and the Seafarers Center. I was afraid I'd forget them. I haven't. I'm happy to share their memories with you.

Some of the other Lykes Guys we were friends with that were still active seafarers at that time were Eddie M, OB and Freddie. I first met Eddie M when he was in the hospital in Galveston. He had been coming into our Seafarers Center for years before I worked there. The day I would have met him in the Center, Eddie M had a terrible accident on his ship. He slipped and fell down the gangway of his ship and severely damaged both legs. After that incident he was forced to retire. He settled back, where he was originally from in Michigan. He was a religious man and travelled often on pilgrimage to shrines in Europe. He sent us postcards from the holy places and once in a while would stop in Galveston to see us and bring us little gifts from his travels. In 2010 I was told that he was in a nursing home dying of pancreatic cancer. Just after Christmas 2010, I received a phone call from his good friend, OB, telling me that Eddie M. died.

OB lived in Galveston when he wasn't sailing. He came into the Center often to have a burger with friends. Eventually OB retired and moved to Wisconsin to be near family. OB still calls us once in a while to see how everyone is doing. He was especially concerned following Hurricane Ike. He has many friends in Galveston and wanted to hear about anyone we mutually know. He's always been a good friend of the Seafarers Center.

And then there was Freddie. He and OB were also good friends. Freddie was a seafarer from Hawaii. He loved spending time in the Center whenever his ship was in port. He often brought us treats from overseas. And whenever he went home to Hawaii on vacation he always returned to Galveston with boxes of chocolate covered macadamia nuts for everyone!

Freddie was the youngest of the group. He suffered a heart attack one day that ended his seafaring career. He kept in touch after his medical retirement. He wrote often from Hawaii and told me of his antics around the island. He liked to make photo copies of comic strips he thought were funny and send them to me to brighten up my day. He was a character and a fun guy.

One night while I was on duty at the Seafarers Center I received a phone call from OB with the news that Freddie had passed away from a heart attack. All of us were shocked and saddened by the news. Freddie was only in his 40s when he died.

The Lykes Guys were always "family" to us at the Seafarers Center.

VALERY

About a year after our arrival in Galveston, a Russian tug started making regular trips into the port from Coatzacoalcos, Mexico. That is when I met a seafarer named Valery. Every ten days his ship came into port and I visited. We had some very interesting conversations. At one point Valery told me he didn't believe in God, yet every time I visited he asked me more questions about God, religion, faith, etc.

One day I asked him why he was so curious about God. He told me his father was very cruel to him as a child and as an adult he avoided his father. His father died when Valery was at sea without him having the chance to make peace with him. He was curious about God and life after death because he wanted to know if he could still communicated with his father. That day Valery and I wrote his father a letter. Valery spoke and I wrote.

The letter was filled with pain and suffering as a child and great regret that things were not resolved while his father was still alive. It went on for pages. Valery felt great relief in writing that letter. I gave it to him to keep in a sacred place.

Over a year later, I was in New Orleans in the St. Louis Cathedral. Valery's guardian angel asked me to pray for him and as I did, I lit a candle for him and his father's soul. A week later I received a letter from him saying he was home in Russia and went into an Orthodox Church. He said he lit a candle for my family there. The date on his letter was the exact date I was in the Cathedral in New Orleans lighting a candle for him and his father. Guardian angels are wonderful and God is totally awesome!

M/V SHEN QUAN HAI

My visit aboard the M/V SHEN QUAN HAI gave three young Chinese seafarers the opportunity to practice their English. Earlier in the day I had taken one of the A/Bs to the store to buy four cases of Coca-Cola. When we arrived back at the ship others were anxious for a visit.

During our conversations, they asked about Galveston, family and other subjects they were interested in. Their English was very broken and it took some deciphering to understand the general ideas in their sentences.

These young men were very good humored and we were all laughing at our communication games. At one point the other A/B asked, "Why are you so kind to us?" "Because you are my brothers!" I replied. For about three seconds I could see him processing my words then with a great big smile he said, "Brother! Yes! I am your brother!" Then he explained in Chinese to the others and they laughed. They all wanted to be brothers too! They said I must have a big family. "Believe me I do!" I told them. My brothers and I conversed for a long time that day. We all enjoyed it very much.

M/V AFRICAN EVERGREEN

On August 21, 1995, aboard the M/V AFRICAN EVERGREEN three Filipino seafarers died as a result of a fire on board as they crossed the Atlantic. Carlito, Boy, and Roderick all lost their lives at sea.

On August 18, 1996, nearly one year later, the three dead seafarers were remembered by their shipmates when the AFRICAN EVERGREEN was in the Port of Galveston.

Some of the crew members were able to attend Mass that morning at St. Patrick Catholic Church with my family and me. Many others, though, had to stay on board to ready the ship for loading the next morning. At the crew's request I held a memorial service aboard the ship that Sunday evening. The Memorial Service was also a Communion Service for those who wanted to receive the Sacrament while in port. At the service, following the gospel, the seafarers spoke about their shipmates who died. It was a beautiful remembrance.

I spent time on board this vessel with the crew the few days that they were in Galveston loading grain. I spoke with all the crew, saw photos of their children and delivered bags of children's clothing for the crew to give to their own children and to the poor in Matadi, Zaire, which was the port in Africa where they were going. At lunchtime I gave out blessed rosaries and talked with them about keeping close to God. They thought about their three shipmates who had died and how life at sea could have them facing such a fate themselves. They wanted to be right with God and family. In November of that year I heard from one of the crew, Roval. He wrote:

Sister Karen,

Hi there! Surprise! I really wanted to write early as possible but time didn't let me. Sorry....

Thanks for the rosary that you have given me. I've learned to talk to God after having known you. I'm praying for my family and your family each time I go to bed. You will always be included in my prayers. It is more powerful, they say, if somebody is praying for you…I'm always practicing to spend ten to twenty minutes with the Lord. I'm very thankful for having a wonderful baby girl and wife. I know He knows how much I feel for them.

Thank you so much.

Love and prayers,

Roval

TVs FOR MATADI

The LOUISIANA oil rig was in dry dock for repair. As they came closer to finishing the work and leaving port, they donated many televisions to our Seafarers Center to be distributed aboard ships. They were getting new ones and wanted the old ones to go to someone who could really use them. The TVs were 220v, which most ships are wired for so many ships' crews were happy with the LOUISIANA's donation.

On the evening of February 2, 1998, our friends on the M/V AFRICAN EVERGREEN came into port. This particular ship sailed from Galveston to Matadi, Zaire often. And often they took children's clothing (stuff my kids out grew but were still like new), bags of rice, candy and other items for the people of Matadi. This was all in addition to their cargo of grain. The seafarers aboard the AFRICAN EVERGREEN said they never saw people as poor as those in Matadi.

The Filipino Chief Officer, Peter, was the man who had

spearheaded this charity for several years. Peter shared what he could with the poor in Africa, often using his own wages to purchase second hand clothes, rice, and medicines. The people of Matadi knew this ship well as the men of Matadi worked as "washers" when the ships docked there.

They washed down the ship to earn enough for food for their families.

The seafarers aboard the AFRICAN EVERGREEN and their sister ships were very sensitive to the needs of the poor in Matadi. Most of the seafarers on board these ships were Filipino.

On the night of February 2 we had exactly four televisions left from the LOUISIANA donation. I asked Peter if the people of Matadi could use them. He smiled broadly, "Oh, they will be so happy!" The next morning Peter and some of his crew unloaded them from our Center van and took them on board to be bound for Matadi later that day.

The crew of the AFRICAN EVERGREEN is a very special one to me. They are loving and caring people. They are carrying the gospel to the ends of the earth! A year before the TVs went to Matadi we lost one of the young ones on board. Leonardo, a young Filipino seafarer, died of malaria. I kept his name on a small piece of paper in the Center's van. Every day I went out to the docks I would see his name and pray for him, his family and his shipmates.

ASH WEDNESDAY

Lent is the time for Christians to prepare for the Passion, Death and Resurrection of our Lord, Jesus Christ. Ash

Wednesday is the beginning of Lent and an important day for all Christians. Catholic Christians have the tradition of receiving ashes on our foreheads.

In preparation for Ash Wednesday, I visit ships that will be sailing before that day that had Catholic seafarers on board who were willing to be ash distributors. I provide them with a small container of blessed ashes and "Way of the Cross at Sea" booklets. They are usually very excited to be able to participate in their Catholic faith tradition at sea.

On Ash Wednesday, I usually board each ship in port and visit as usual, but also explain that I am carrying ashes with me. Many crewmembers come to hear me speak about Lent. Mostly the Catholics received the ashes, but one time a Muslim from Indonesia asked for the ashes as well. He said he believes in one God and wanted to be close to God through our tradition. On another occasion, a Protestant Filipino didn't come for the ashes but to receive a Way of the Cross at Sea booklet. Others have told me about or showed me the prayer booklets they keep in their cabins with special prayers such as novenas. I see pictures from shrines they visited and hear stories about walking in the Holy Land where "Jesus walked" when their ships were in Israel.

Ash Wednesday for me is a joyous day because I see the pride and love so many seafarers have in their faith. They may be far from home and their home parishes, but the light of Jesus burns bright in their hearts. They are in position to spread the gospel to the ends of the earth, if we fan the flames burning inside them. They must know that praying alone inside their cabins is beautiful, but praying together as a shipboard prayer community will strengthen their faith and spread it to others. Seafarers are God's gift to all of us on land.

M/V CHIOS DREAM

In 1997 the CHIOS DREAM came to Galveston to discharge sugar in mid January. When I boarded the vessel, I was surprised to see my friend, Petros, a 2nd officer from Greece. I had known Petros for four years at that point as he sailed into Galveston on vessels from the "Golden" line. I didn't know that he had changed companies.

Petros and I spent the morning catching up on things. He filled me in on his mother and father, the progress of the house he is building, and his plans for the future. It had been two years since he came to Galveston, but we have kept in touch by letter.

I met other officers and crew on board and in the Seafarers Center during their stay. On the morning of their last day in port, Captain Sofoklis came to me with an unusual request. His wife, Silvia, was travelling with him. They had been married six years but were unable to have children so far. Silvia had gone through some surgery prior to her sailing with Sofoklis. She had been on board two months when the ship came to Galveston and was suspecting she was pregnant now, so the Captain asked me to find a doctor to confirm it that day before their afternoon sailing time.

After a few phone calls I was able to find a Galveston doctor willing to work her in for a pregnancy test. In the waiting room, I waited with Petros and another officer while the Captain and his wife went in for the exam. The other women in the waiting room got the idea of what was happening from our conversation. After a little while the Captain emerged beaming with delight, "I'm going to be a 'Popi'!" Everyone said, "Opah!" Even the women in the waiting room cheered!

We stopped on the way back to the ship to buy cake and champagne (cake for 'Mama', champagne for 'Popi' and everyone else) for the celebration of new life. Lunch that day was filled with excitement. Silvia was scheduled to leave the ship in New Orleans to go home to Greece to be under the doctor's care.

Petros and I had one last talk before the ship left. It was a joy-filled time.

M/V MARINE DUVALL

There is a name plate from a ship named the MARINE DUVALL that hangs in our Seafarers Center. The name plate used to be bolted above the bridge deck of the American flagged bulk ship. Several years ago, when the MARINE DUVALL was taking her last voyage to be scrapped, someone asked if we would like her name plate for our Seafarers Center. You bet we did!

For many years the MARINE DUVALL sailed between Galveston and Tampa on a regular run. Over those years we got to know crew members well. Whenever the MARINE DUVALL was in port I went to visit. Sometimes I was well received and sometimes I was made to feel like I was intruding. Just being present in the mess room caused a whole gambit of reactions. I experienced everything from cheerful, "Hey, Chaplain!" greetings to guys nearly knocking me over trying to get out of the room before they felt they had to talk to me.

After greeting and spending time with the seafarers who were happy to see me, I still made my way into the television room to say hello again to the ones who ran out of the mess. Usually they just cursed and left the room, but there were several times over the years that one would stay behind and slowly begin to talk. Almost always that one person would have some serious problem to pour out. And always I would listen.

The seafarers aboard the MARINE DUVALL had a special place in my heart. I never let the grumpy guys keep me away. I never forced anyone to stay in the same room and talk with me. I just made myself present. Eventually those who needed me to be there for them understood I was there for them.

During that time, my spiritual director told me to find a walking stick to represent prayer. He said to use the symbol of a walking stick to remember that prayer is my stability along the journey of life. I searched and searched for a suitable walking stick but could not fine one. This went on for months.

One of the MARINE DUVALL seafarers I helped is named William. William had a bad drinking problem back when I visited him on the ship. He was going through a difficult divorce and custody battle. He was in danger of losing his job due to excessive drinking. I worked with him for weeks visiting the ship every time they were in port. Finally William agreed to enter Alcoholics Anonymous and eventually cleaned up. He was truly grateful.

Months later I was on night duty at the Seafarers Center when a family from Houston walked in. The man told me he was William's AA sponsor. He said William told them all about me and how I never gave up on him. Then he handed me a beautiful hand-carved wooded walking stick. He said, "William asked me to give this to you as a thank you. I know it's strange but he said he wanted you to have it." I was stunned. I searched for a walking stick for months and here it was in my hand. That walking stick now graces a corner in our home where I can see it and remember that prayer is my steadying strength along the path God has given me to travel.

A long while after that walking stick was delivered to me, William stopped in the Seafarers Center to see me. When he walked in the front door and greeted me I told him to look up. He saw the MARINE DUVALL name plate hanging there. He smiled a great big smile and said it was where it should be.

RITCHIE BOY

When I was in the Philippines in 1997, I met many young seafaring cadets from the maritime academy at the University in Cebu. Among this group, Ritchie Boy was one of several who have kept in touch over the years. I remember sitting on top of the mountain in Cebu with the cadets watching the sun set over the city below. It was beautiful and peaceful and very spiritual. We prayed together and talked on that mountain top for many hours.

Like the others, Ritchie finished school and set sail to build his career at sea. I received many letters from him along the way. He was very happy to be home after his first vessel as a cadet. He wrote in July 1999:

Dear Ate,

It is nice to be home. I am home with my parents in Camotes Island. I'll spend two months of vacation after 14 months on board. I wish to see you again. I miss you a lot and thank you for all the letters and pictures of the Center and your family you sent to me on board.

You know, Ate, you give me strength to face this salty life. We'll be having our National Seafarers Day in September and I'll volunteer at the Stella Maris Center in Cebu for preparation.

You have a special place in my heart. Until then include us always in your prayers.

Miss you. Ritchie

Ritchie wrote from his second vessel in 2000 and surprised me with some news:

Hello, Ate Karen,

How's life now? How's your family and your Apostolate? Well I am boarded my second vessel last April 30 in Hong Kong. A brand new container vessel. We are mixed nationals. We are only three Filipinos on board, two oilers and one chief officer. Others are German, Russian, and Tuvalu.

Ate, please pray for me. It is my first time to work as oiler from cadet and never been wiper. All are good people here but they don't speak English well. Sometimes when we work together we do only sign language.

My plans next year when I finish my contract is to study again. I would like to go to the seminary. Please pray for me.

Ritchie

I am always praying for Ritchie and all the other cadets that I have met along the way and all the cadets I haven't met as well. The young ones; the future.

"GOOD-BYE, MY PRINCESS"

In early August of 2004, I was visited by Captain Gordan. He comes to see me whenever he is in Galveston. We became good friends when he was master of the M/V CREDA when it served as a cement silo ship in Galveston from December 1998 to February 2002. It was berthed at pier 28 for just over three years. During that time the officers and crew became just like family.

I spent many hours aboard the CREDA over those three years. Sometime I would spend it in the mess with the crew, sometime I'd be in the officer's mess for their coffee break, sometime I'd spend talking with Captain Gordan or Captain Alan (his relief captain) in the office. There were times when we'd have a barbecue on the aft deck in the evenings and we would celebrate birthdays and special occasions together.

Every time a cement ship would tie up to the CREDA to discharge I'd visit the CREDA crew first then climb across to the cement ship to visit that crew. It was a great experience getting to know the seafarers of the CREDA.

Early on, at their first Easter with us, I held a Communion Service aboard ship and gave Captain Gordan a crucifix as a gift. He placed it in his office. On February 9, 2002 I stood on the dock at pier 28 and watched as the CREDA pulled up her lines to leave. All who could be on deck were on deck and I watched until they were out of sight. It really was a very sad day.

The CREDA went to Greece to wait for her next assignment. Over two years passed which brings us to where I started this story: Captain Gordan's visit in 2004. It was great to see him, but his sadness was evident. He told me he just got back from sailing the CREDA on her final voyage. His orders from the company were to sail her to Bangladesh and beach her for scrap. He had a Romanian crew for the final trip, all new guys. It was a very difficult thing for him to do. He was her master for fourteen years.

He described the voyage through the Indian Ocean as ominous. The sea and sky were pitch black and eerie still. There was nothing positive about this voyage and as they neared Bangladesh, his uneasiness increased. As land came into view the sight was overwhelming…it was literally a graveyard of beached ships. There were hundreds of ships stripped and rusting along the shore line.

The nearer they got the more uneasy he became. They were cleared to steam ahead and ram the beach. As the CREDA sailed her last few yards Captain Gordan gently said, "Good-bye, my princess." She ground to a stop and immediately hundreds of Bangladeshi people swarmed the ship to begin stripping her for scrap. He gathered his belongings and went to the office where he removed the crucifix on the wall and tucked it in his bag. He and the crew left the ship and made their way to the airport to go home to their own countries.

I felt sad for Captain Gordan. None of his regular crew was with him on the CREDA for her last voyage. The Romanians were strangers to him and the ship. He was her Master for fourteen years and watched her die alone. But just like a lost loved one, his memories of her are grand.

ELA

Ela, the wife of a Polish seafarer, and I have been friends for many years. We met in 1990 when I was studying at the Houston International Port Chaplaincy School and she was sailing with her husband. His ship came into the Port of Houston that February and I met Ela and others from the ship when they visited the Houston International Seafarers Center one night that I had duty.

Ela and I began corresponding immediately after that. She wrote me whenever her husband was at sea. We exchanged news about our children and discussed situations in our countries and regions. We became good friends.

In June of 2006 the Apostleship of the Sea World Congress took place in Gdynia, Poland. I travelled there with our US delegation. After checking into the hotel and settling into my room, I received a phone call from the front desk saying that I had visitors in the lobby. I hurried down there to find Ela smiling holding a bouquet of yellow roses. It was wonderful to see her again after so many years! We hugged each other and she handed me the roses. There were sixteen roses, one for each year we had corresponded!

Ela's son and his girlfriend came with her. Her husband was at sea. They came to take me to their home for dinner. What a joy it was for me to spend time with my friend, Ela, and her family in their home for the very first time!

THE POPE, BRANDO, AND ME

I met Brando when he joined his first cruise ship back in 1993. It was the STAR OF TEXAS that home ported in Galveston. It was his first time away from home and he started his cruise ship career by dragging garbage off the ship every day when it returned to port from its day cruises. Sometimes the only time we could find to talk was when I spent days walking with him as he and others dragged tons of garbage from the ship to the dumpsters.

Back then, Brando was homesick but was determined to work hard and make an honest living to keep his family safe from the drug wars in Colombia. Brando and I have been corresponding since then. He's had a very hard life. His dream was to immigrate to Canada or the United States to help his family. So far he hasn't been able to do that.

We have corresponded, mostly through email, over the years. In 1998, Brando wrote from his ship:

Hello, Hermana, How are you doing? It's just a short note to say hello and let you know I am okay. I will stay with the ship about two more weeks and next 28 November I'll be back home. I hope to get mail from you and let you know how everything is back home. I have to tell you that I met Father Lee Smith [the port chaplain for Brooklyn, NY] in the middle of the Atlantic on board our vessel. He knows you! God Bless You – Brando

In August of 1999 Brando wrote from the sea:

Hello, Sister Karen, how are you and all the seafarers? Did they miss you when you went on vacation? Of course they did!
I want to tell you what happened this morning in my hometown. My Uncle Ricardo was almost murdered when he was going to his farm in the country. Somebody was hiding and shot him in the back. ...They found him but the doctors in our town could not help him. They had to drive him to a hospital six hours away, so at this moment I don't know what happened.
Sister, please pray for him. I will tell you later what has happened. God bless you, Hermana. Brando

I immediately began to pray for Uncle Ricardo. And I waited for more news from Brando. I knew he would be so worried and yet he still had to work long hours and concentrate on his work. Nearly a week later I received another email from Brando. It said:

Hola, Hermana Karen,
Thanks so much for your prayers. Thank God my uncle is better and hopefully he will be back home soon. I ask you to keep praying for his health, that nothing bring secondary damages. You are in my prayers, Sister.

In mid 2003, Brando joined a Spanish cruise ship operating in the Mediterranean Sea. Regardless what it looks like to passengers, cruise ship jobs are very hard. The competition for jobs is fierce, the prejudice between and among nationalities is great, and the pressure to "please the passengers" or be replaced can be crushing. All these factors began to take their toll on Brando. At the end of October of that year I opened an email from him saying:

Sister, I think I am losing my will to live. Please pray for me.

Immediately I emailed him back promising prayers. Then I emailed the people I knew would help me to pray for him immediately. Daily I prayed and emailed him. I heard nothing back from him for a week. I hoped it was because the ship was at sea and he had no email access.

About a week later, I received an email again from Brando. He was overwhelmed by all the emails and prayers he received. He said he felt the strength from the prayers. When the ship arrived in Malta, he went ashore and found a church in which he had a long talk with the priest there. He went to confession and received Holy Communion. He was feeling stronger and more able to handle the hard life on board. He said, *"The power of prayer is awesome!"*

In mid August, 2004, to my delight, Brando called me from Rome where his ship was docked. He was on a regular run in the Mediterranean Sea. It was the first time we spoke by phone since I saw him last in 1993.

I asked him how things were on this new vessel. He was quiet. I asked him what was wrong. He said he called just to talk again. He said the emails are nice, but he really missed our dockside talks. I knew something was very wrong. After some prompting he confided in me that he was exhausted. He was a bartender on this vessel and his work schedule was from 10am to 6am seven days a week. He was on board for two months at that point and had four months to go. He didn't think he could make it. But he didn't call for me to help him. If he complained he would lose his job. If he stayed on board he risked losing his health. He asked me only to pray for him.

Brando's story is not unique. The stories of cruise ship workers are not well known to the sailing public. Passengers often comment on how much their waiters smile and how pleasant the staff was during their cruise. There are so many people waiting for jobs on cruise ships that it is in the best interest of the workers who have the jobs to be pleasant all the time- even when they only get four hours off per day.

I think of Brando every time we have a cruise ship in port and whisper a prayer for him and all who suffer to support their families with jobs on the sea. It certainly isn't an easy life.

Brando's problems on board became so overwhelming he needed help. It happened that I met a priest from Colombia while staying at the Scalabrini House in Rome on my trip there in 2004. I emailed Fr. Carlos when Brando needed help and I asked him if he would contact Brando. First Fr. Carlos emailed Brando on board. He explained that he was a friend of mine and that he was studying in Rome. He asked

Brando if he would like to meet when his ship docked in Chivitaveccia (near Rome). They made a plan to meet.

Brando later emailed me:

Hermana, it was a wonderful gift from you! You got us in contact with each other by email and we got together in Rome one whole day. We talked for long hours, he took me to a nice non-touristic church where we prayed together…beautiful moments. You were aware of every single moment, you kept writing me to support me, you put me in contact with this priest and he was also there to strengthen me! Thank you for being there in such moments!

In 2006, Brando was sailing on another cruise ship that called into the port of Rome. Through email I told him that I would be in Rome that October and if his cruise ship was in port at that time we could try to meet again after thirteen years. He was excited about that.

After receiving my itinerary we discovered, indeed, that I would be in Rome the same time his ship had a port call there. October 27, 2006. This was great news. The last time Brando was in Galveston he was only nineteen years old. We had corresponded ever since. We made a plan to meet in St. Peter's Square at 11:00 am near the first column on the right facing the Basilica.

So, on October 27 I took the bus into town and walked to St. Peter's Square. I stood by the first column on the right and waited. Brando had to take a train from the port to get into town. I was standing facing the street when Pope John Paul II's motorcade passed by. It was Wednesday and the Holy

Father was going to have a general audience in St. Peter's Square. There were tens of thousands of people there. How would I ever find him?

It was quarter past eleven and still I didn't see him. The crowds were rushing to get into the square. The Pope began speaking. I crossed the street and found a pay phone. I called Brando's cell phone number. He answered and I asked him where he was. He said he was in St. Peter's Square at the first column on the right. I told him I was just there and didn't see him. He described what he could see from where he was standing. He was seeing what I was seeing. I hung up the phone and went back to the pillar. No Brando.

The Pope was on the steps of St. Peter's in the Square speaking now. People were everywhere! I finally just asked our guardian angels to guide us. Right then I turned around and at that same moment the man who had been standing behind me turned around. We had been standing back to back! Brando threw up his arms and yelled, "My sister Karen is in Rome with me and the Pope!" And then it began a gentle rain. What a great blessing! The last time we visited together and walked the docks in Galveston thirteen years earlier we were standing on Pier 25 talking in a gentle rain. Brando looked up to the sky and said, "Thank you, God!"

Brando, the Pope and Me

We spent the next few hours visiting in Rome. It was just like meeting up with my brother. Brando and I have corresponded all these years so we know about each other's families and work. We didn't have to catch up on thirteen years, we only had to enjoy the day.

After lunch, Brando said he wanted to go to the Trevi Fountain, the famous fountain in Rome where you toss a coin if you wish to return. So we took a bus to Trevi Fountain and tossed in a coin. As we sat among the tourists looking at the fountain, Brando said, "Do you remember when I was so sick in Galveston and you took me to the doctor?" Yes, I remember. He said, "Thank you for being my big sister."

All too soon the time passed. Brando had to catch his train back to the port and I had to catch a bus to my next meeting. It was raining again when we said good-bye. That was good because it hid my tears.

"DADDY IS GOING TO LIVE WITH GENIUS"

Joy is an American ship captain. I've known her since she was a cadet at Texas A&M Maritime Academy in Galveston in the early 1990s. We have corresponded for years. Joy had her struggles. In a letter I received from her in January, 1996 she wrote:

Hi Karen!

Your letters always enlighten and touch me in a positive way! Thanks for the constant response; you are one of the few whom I can count on to actually write back…I've begun to pray a lot for many things- a new job, health, safety, and family.

Thanks again,

Joy

About ten years after we met, Joy met her soul mate, Jonathan, another ship captain. They married and soon started their family. When Joy was eight months pregnant with their daughter, Sally, Jonathan was diagnosed with a brain tumor. For nearly four years he fought through chemotherapy and radiation and whatever other treatments the doctors were willing to try.

Joy was raised Roman Catholic but slowly moved away from the Church. She never stopped believing, she just didn't practice her faith. Throughout Jonathan's illness I watched both of them grow in faith. They drew strength from Jesus and the angels. And when it became apparent that the treatments weren't working they surrendered themselves to God.

Jonathan entered hospice care the beginning of December 2007. I had the blessing of being his hospice chaplain. Their daughter, Sally, then three and a half years old, only knew her Daddy to be sick. She sat on his bed and checked his pulse like she saw the nurses do. She looked at the crucifix on the wall and said, "Daddy is going to live with Genius," which is what she called Jesus.

On the night of December 22, the doorbell at their home rang. Jonathan was nearing the end of his time here on earth. Joy opened the front door to find many of their neighbors singing the most sacred of Christmas hymns. She felt the room fill with peace and she opened the door wide so Jonathan, who was lying on a hospital bed in the living room, could hear them. Joy stood there feeling the presence of God and the peace of His promise. Jonathan died peacefully a few hours later.

FROM BULGARIA WITH LOVE

Hurricane Ike destroyed our Seafarers Center in Galveston and many homes and businesses on the island on September 13, 2008. The initial shock of seeing the devastation was overwhelming and depressing. In the process of immediate action we had to open a post office box to receive our redirected mail. Daily I went to the post office in League City (Galveston's post office was indefinitely closed) to check for mail for the Seafarers Center. One day I went there and found a note in the box that a package had arrived. I took the note to the desk and was handed the package. It was addressed to my family and the return address was in Bulgaria.

I took the box home and curiously opened it. I found it filled with many non-perishable food items and pretzels, cheese curls, chocolate, other snacks, and some souvenirs from Bulgaria. There was a note inside the box from a seafarer's wife named Mariana. The note said she heard about the hurricane and was worried about us. She wished us a fast and easy recovery. She continued, *"I hope so that Seafarers Center soon will be rebuilt and working as before Ike. I wish you and your family health and courage facing the challenges that life sends us."*

Why was this package so special? (And, yes, it did make me cry). It was about six years earlier that I met Mariana's husband, Angel. He was aboard a ship that had all Chinese officers and crew. He was the only Bulgarian on board. When they arrived in Galveston I went to visit the ship and in the mess room Angel quietly told me he was very hungry. He said the Chinese were discriminating against him and were spitting and urinating in his food. He refused to eat unless he was able to prepare his own food in the galley. He wasn't part of the galley crew so he was not allowed in the kitchen.

My first priority was to get the man some food. My second priority was to get him removed from the vessel safely. It happened that it was one of very few cold days in Galveston during the winter months. I was able to wear an over-sized trench coat without suspicion. Under the coat I hid a roasted chicken, a loaf of French bread, a container of cooked kielbasa and sour kraut, and some fruit and vegetables. Carefully I slipped those things to Angel one by one to put in his cabin.

Back at my office I did some calling around to try and get him signed off in Galveston so he wouldn't have to sail with the ship. Unfortunately the best I could do was the promise of getting him signed off in the next port in Mexico. So that meant I had to get more food on board for him to store in his cabin. The second trip to his ship with food I had hidden in the lining of my coat many cans of vegetables, a can opener, tuna, and a box of crackers. By the time the vessel left for Mexico, Angel had a good stash of food in his cabin. And, as promised, he was able to sign off the ship in Mexico and go home.

Angel told his family how I fed him when he was hungry. So when his wife, Mariana, heard about the hurricane in Galveston, she wanted to make sure my family had food. That is why the box was sent with whatever she could find to keep kids' stomachs from being hungry. What a touching gift and what a blessing this ministry has been in my life.

ALEXANDRE'S DAUGHTER

I met Alexandre in 1991 when Russia was still part of the Soviet Union. He was aboard a bulk ship that called in the Port of Detroit, Michigan, where I was serving at the time. And, although, there were Soviet commissars on board on all their ships back then, Alexandre and I had the unique chance to become friends.

I took him and some of his shipmates, including the commissar, to a thrift store for shopping. As everyone got out of the van and walked through the parking lot to the store, Alexandre stayed behind. The commissar didn't notice.

He then asked me if we could take a walk through the neighborhood nearby instead of going shopping. So that is what we did.

He knew it was risky to do if the commissar noticed he was missing, but he longed to see life as it was in America. As we walked along through the neighborhood we saw people doing their everyday kind of things. There was a woman gardening, an older man watering his grass. Some children ran past us squealing as they chased each other. Then a little girl squeaked past us on her tricycle. Alexandre said she reminded him of his toddler, Lisa.

We walked and talked for three hours that day. He spoke about life in the Soviet Union and the difficulties of getting simple things like baby formula or diapers. The lack of good health care left his wife with serious infections after each child was born. He confided in me that he didn't want to go shopping because he didn't have the money to shop. As a 4th officer he only made US$100 a month. Most of that he sent home to his family. But no matter how bleak things looked he always spoke with hope that their lives would get better.

Lisa and her Husband, Valery

Ever since that one and only time we met, Alexandre and I have corresponded. The first photo he sent me was when he went home from that ship. It was a photo of him holding his daughter, Lisa. They were in winter coats and she had a knit cap on her head. Her cheeks were rosy from the cold and in the background their surroundings were covered in snow. He looked so happy in that photo. It was one of my favorite seafarer family photos.

Over the years we exchanged photos of our children as they grew. In February of 2009 a letter arrived from Alexandre. The envelope was heavy. When I opened it I found many photos of Lisa's wedding. What a joy to see this beautiful young lady all grown up! There were photos of her with Alexandre and her mother and sister, Katya, as well as her new husband.

I read his letter expressing grief over the loss of our Seafarers Center in the hurricane and that he wanted to share the joy of their daughter's wedding with us to give us a happy thought in this difficult time. It was then I realized I lost all of Lisa and Katya's baby pictures and so many, many more photos of other seafarers' families. The joy of seeing the wedding photos gave way to the grief of losing the other precious treasures. I was in the safety of my home with my husband nearby and I sobbed deeply over this loss.

There were thousands of letters from seafarers and their families in my office as well as thousands of photos of the families that were all lost in the flood. Lost were not just pieces of paper but pieces of the lives of the people I served for nearly a quarter century.

Our Seafarers Center was closed for 14 months while we cleaned it out, began the reconstruction and were finally able to open on a part time basis as further construction took place. Now, I am able to look at the photos of Lisa's wedding and rejoice again with them. Time does heal all wounds.

BILLY'S ANGEL

I met Billy in 1994 on the streets of Galveston. He is an American seafarer born and raised in Galveston. When I first met Billy he was a dying drug addict on the streets. After several weeks of talking with him, praying for him, and being in communication with his union officials, Billy finally asked for help getting into rehab. In September 1994, he left Galveston and was flown to Maryland by the union to enter their drug and alcohol rehab program.

Billy did very well and re-entered society as a productive person. He shipped back out, made a good living, and gave back to his community through monetary donations and volunteer work. When his elderly mother took ill he became her primary care giver. It was wonderful to see Billy as his real self and no longer just a shell filled with drugs.

Billy's mother died in 2003, just days before my own father died. That was very hard on him. A couple of other family events depressed him even more and by 2005 sadly he turned back to drugs to numb the pain. We had to exercise "tough love" at the Seafarers Center not allowing him to enter to protect others and to send Billy a message that he needed to get help. He floundered for two years. He forgot that I always knew when he was lying. Finally he hit bottom again and crawled back for help. Again the union took him into rehab. Everyone there knows what kind of person Billy can be when he is clean.

Billy stayed in Maryland at the rehab center for a year. He was there at first to go through the program and then to help others coming in after him. He was there when Hurricane Ike hit Galveston and he worried about us, his surrogate family.

One day in late May 2009, Billy called to say he was coming back to Houston in June. He was in contact with the union and there was a job waiting for him on a ship. He came back to the union hall in Houston to get all the paperwork done. On Thursday, June 11th, the North American Maritime Ministry Association Conference was coming to a close in Houston. Port chaplains and Seafarers Center directors from all over North America and the Caribbean had descended on Houston for a three day conference that week. The closing ecumenical worship service was scheduled to take place at the new Co-Cathedral of the Archdiocese of Galveston-Houston downtown. I knew Billy was over at the Union Hall that day which is nearby the Co-Cathedral. I wanted to call him to come over to the Cathedral for the service because I knew it would be good for him. I discovered I didn't have his cell phone number with me and couldn't find it in my phone's caller ID. I started to pray for help. I asked Jesus to help me find Billy's phone number. Well, Jesus did one better.

Billy with my Children

As I stood in the vestibule of the Co-Cathedral looking through the numbers on my caller ID for a third time, the door of the cathedral opened and in walked a bewildered Billy. He saw me there and said, "What are you doing here, Sis?" I explained why I was there and that I had been trying to find his phone number to call him to come over. I told him I was praying to find the number. He said he was at the union hall and had an urge to go for a walk. As he passed by the Co-Cathedral he felt an even stronger urge to open the door and walk in. We both looked at each other and said, "Guardian angel." When all else fails guardian angels are the fastest way to get messages to people.

Billy sat next to me during the service. The Scripture readings were all about God being with those who were in raging seas, blessing people who work on the sea. Daniel Cardinal DiNardo, the shepherd of the Archdiocese of Galveston-Houston, gave the homily. It was a wonderful message. I saw Billy fill with grace and tears welled up in his eyes. He felt loved by the strength of God that day. And I knew he would join his next vessel with the strength and grace he needed to enter back into his life at sea.

Billy had another set back on his road to recovery but is once again back at sea. We pray that he continues to get up and keep walking whenever he falls. That is all God asks of any of us.

SAMPATH

Our Seafarers Center was still closed for repair following Hurricane Ike when I received an email from Pat Poulos, the Director of the Houston International Seafarers Center, telling me that a Sri Lankan cadet was air lifted to the Mainland Medical Center in Texas City after receiving a critical burn aboard his tanker vessel in the Gulf of Mexico. The University of Texas Medical Branch (our hospital in Galveston) was heavily damaged in the hurricane and was not accepting burn patients.

I went to the hospital in Texas City and found the young seafarer, Sampath, already there for approximately two weeks and had undergone a few surgeries. Sampath was an engine room cadet aboard a foreign tanker.

The Mainland Medical Center does not have a burn unit. The doctors there worked to save his hand, but burns are not their specialty. Sampath underwent multiple surgeries. He was in severe and constant pain.

When I began visiting him in late August, the nurses told me he wasn't eating. I asked permission to bring in foods that he would like. American hospital food is difficult for someone who is used to more spicy foods. The doctors said to try it. At first I tried to cook some Sri Lankan food. Twice I brought in dishes I made for him. He ate it but not very enthusiastically. So reaching out into the community the Sri Lankan-American families in the area really stepped up and adopted Sampath. Daily and sometimes twice a day he was brought home cooked Sri Lankan meals. He was able to visit with people who spoke his language. The Buddhist priest from the temple in Houston visited regularly.

Once his food situation was under control, my main focus became helping him cope with the pain. I spent hours beside his bed getting him to talk about his family, his childhood, his Buddhist faith, and anything else that would distract him from the intense pain. His pain levels could go from a 9 down to a 3 or 4 just by getting him to talk and think about silly things he did when he was a boy. I also tried to get him to watch a little TV to distract his mind. He liked the nature channel and so we watched birds or lions or whatever was on and talk about them. It seemed to help.

On September 25th he endured a surgery that removed a muscle from his back to try and reconstruct his fingers. Sampath spent the weekend in the Intensive Care Unit. His pain was extreme. I stayed by his side.

One day he was particularly having a rough day. I was flipping through the channels on the TV desperate to find something to help ease his mind. And there is was– an old Tom and Jerry cartoon on the cartoon channel. There are no words in those cartoons, just a cat chasing a mouse and a mouse doing silly things to get away from the cat. It made Sampath laugh. It was a good distraction.

On the 27th of September Sampath celebrated his 26th birthday. It could have been a very sad and lonely day for him. Instead, he was not alone. Families from all over the area came to spend time with him. There were balloons, cake, photos, singing. The gift from my family was a two DVD disc set of Tom and Jerry cartoons. Sampath once again laughed. He felt the love of our community and it is something he will never forget.

A few days after his birthday, Sampath had surgery again. This time it was to see how well the muscle was grafting to the bones. The doctors were very optimistic. Sampath was so happy he began calling people, first his mother! His whole demeanor changed. The news meant his chance of having his fingers amputated decreased tremendously.

On October 2, I found the occupational therapist in his room working with him, helping him to slowly start to stretch his back, his arm and wrist. He began working hard to recover. He still faced more surgeries. Skin was taken from his abdomen and his thighs to graft onto his hand. He said his hand looked like a "monster hand". The doctor told him the swelling would eventually go down, and the large muscle from his back that is now part of his fingers would be trimmed.

One day Sampath and I had a long talk. He told me how in his young life he has been in many situations in which he has escaped death. For instance, just a year before his accident on the ship his classmates from the maritime academy and he were at the harbor doing some studies when a bomb went off in an area they had just left. The year before that, a bomb went off right at the maritime academy and twenty of his fellow cadets had been killed. He just left that particular building a few minutes earlier. And when the giant tsunami hit the Sri Lankan coast, Sampath had been in a village on the coast for holiday and just boarded a bus heading back to the capital. Fifteen minutes after the bus left, the seaside village was wiped out by the tidal wave. He feels fortunate that God spared his life so many times.

On November 2, 2009, after seventy-eight days and sixteen surgeries, Sampath flew home to Sri Lanka for further treatment and to figure out what his future would be. On Christmas Day he called me from Sri Lanka. He said, *"Merry Christmas! I will never forget you, Sister. All that time you spent sitting with me. No never. My family knows you well now too because I keep your photo nearby and tell them all about you."*

Sampath, his wife Kushi and their Newborn Son

He and his girlfriend, Kushi, who eventually became his wife, continue to keep in touch via email. I continue to send him cards and encouraging letters. I received another phone call from Sampath while I was waiting for a plane at the airport in Buffalo, New York in May 2010. He thanked me for all the letters. He said it helps keep him from being depressed. He knows he has a long way to go before he can use his hand and work again. Then he said, *"When I was in the hospital in Texas it was the most painful time of my life but it was also the happiest time in my life because I felt the genuine love of strangers. I never experienced that before. I remember, Sister, when you came to the hospital at 6:00am before my surgeries and* sat with me for hours when I was in so much pain. If it wasn't for you, Sister, I would not be here."

I am very happy I was able to be there for him when he needed me most. Sampath and his girlfriend, Kushi, have since gotten married and recently sent me a photo of the latest edition to their family, a son named Savinu. Life goes on!

WILSON

On Sunday, January 24, 2010, a horrible accident took place on a ship at anchor in the Gulf of Mexico. 2nd Engineer, Wilson and motorman, Carlos, were working on a steam valve in the engine room when it opened up on them and blew them back. Wilson took the brunt of the steam and had third degree burns over 90% of his body. Carlos sustained second and third degree burns on his left leg, left arm, chest and neck. Both men were from Ecuador.

I received a call asking me to please get a priest to the University of Texas Medical Branch's burn unit, which was finally open again after months of being closed following Hurricane Ike. It happened that Fr. John Paul from Holy Family Parish in Galveston was at UTMB making his rounds. I caught up with him and was able to get him over to see Wilson and anoint him. Meanwhile I went to visit Carlos.

Carlos was going to be fine. He had burns that would heal well and he was expected to be in the hospital about three weeks. Wilson's story is not so happy. The shipping company began the process of getting his wife a visa to be able to come to Galveston and be with him. As she was trying to get an emergency visa in Ecuador, Wilson's oldest sister,

Maria, arrived from Philadelphia where she lives. Maria's two daughters also travelled with her. They were devastated to see him in the burn unit.

In my nearly 30 years of ministry and countless trips to the hospital to visit injured or ill seafarers, the burn unit remains the most difficult place to go. But in all my years of visiting seafarers in the burn unit all of them survived. Wilson, though, was the most critical.

As days passed, his wife, Paulina and brother, Dalton arrived from Ecuador. His sister, Martha arrived soon after. The family clung to any small pieces of hope they could find. The nurses told them that Wilson could hear them and encouraged them to speak to him. Paulina spoke to him and he gave a reaction. His blood pressure spiked. Whenever I visited him I would recite the rosary aloud so he could hear the peaceful cadence of prayers. His nurse asked me one day if I was praying for them too. I told her the prayers were for all who were caring for him and all the patients in the burn unit and families. She was happy.

I visited the hospital daily and spent time with the family. There were other families in the waiting room too and each became supports for the other. It was beautiful. Fr. John Paul came several times a week to pray with Wilson and pray with his family. They found great comfort in his visits. The doctors worked heroically to try to save him. Unfortunately, nature took its course.

Infections began to set in and slowly Wilson's organs began shutting down. On the afternoon of February 22, Wilson died. Pauline was inconsolable. She was thinking of their two young sons, Paulo and Wilson- ages six and three. The children were being cared for by Paulina's parents in Ecuador. Maria had, just that morning, looked at her brother with all the tubes and wires hooked up to machines and a respirator breathing for him, and all the bloody gauze covering his burns and said, "Jesus, I trust you. You know what he needs." For three weeks she watched him slowly fail. She was at peace in letting him go.

The Wednesday following Wilson's death I was with the family at the funeral home as they made arrangements to have his body sent home. His body arrived from the hospital on a gurney in a body bag. It was the first time we saw him after his death. It was a sad and traumatic viewing. No more tubes, no more gauze and bandages. I was happy to be there for them, although it was one of the hardest things I've had to do as a chaplain.

Deacon Henry from Holy Family Parish came to the funeral home to discuss the funeral arrangements with the family in Spanish. They were grateful for his help. On the evening of March 2, we had a simple dinner for the family at the Seafarers Center as they prepared to go home. The dinner was attended by our staff and board members.

Fr. John Paul gave the blessing followed by Wilson's brother, Dalton, offering the family's thanks for all the Seafarers Center did for them while they were here. There wasn't a dry eye in the room after his heartfelt words but we were able to enjoy a wonderful meal together.

Wilson's body was flown home on March 3. On March 14 we received the following email from his family:

Hello Dear Karen,

This is Martha and Paulina. Paulina and Dalton got here to Quito a day after Wilson's body arrived. As you know, in most of the funeral, we were sad and happy. Sad because of the situation and happy because we saw friends and family that we have stopped seen many many years ago. Wilson was loved, that we knew even before his death and those people who were with us showed their love for him. Paulina and some of his brothers stayed over night with him and on the next day we had a beautiful Mass with people singing beautifully as well as a cousin who sang two songs that reminded us of Wilson's love for our home town. Then in the afternoon, we buried his ashes under the tree that his little sons picked out for him. We are trying to get over this. I know he would want that. Thank you for everything you did for us and for Wilson.

Martha and Paulina

FROM CADET TO CAPTAIN

On Friday, March 12, my cell phone rang and I heard a voice I hadn't heard in twenty years say, "May I please speak with Mrs. Karen Parsons?" "This is Karen Parsons," I answered. "This is Captain Marek." The next thing out of my mouth was something like, "AHHHHHHHHHHHH! I can't believe it!"

Although I hadn't seen or heard him in twenty years, we have communicated via snail mail since we met in 1990. When we first met, Marek was a twenty year old cadet from Poland. I was attending the Houston Port Chaplaincy

School working toward my chaplain certification. Marek's ship was in port in Houston then. Marek and I had a very long conversation when I had night duty. I later used my conversation with Marek as one of my CPE (Clinical Pastoral Education) verbatims.

The time period in history was when Germany was beginning unification talks and the coming down of the Berlin Wall. As a young Polish man about to get married Marek had a genuine fear of Germany reuniting. After all, Poland's borders have changed time and again when others have invaded, especially Germany. He asked how the US could help in assuring Poland that a German reunification would be okay. I knew our country was also concerned and so I contacted the senators on the Foreign Relations Committee, told them about the conversation I had with Marek and asked them what the US was doing in this process. I received several responses indicating that the US would be in on the reunification talks and would take Marek's concerns along with others of Poland to the table.

I wrote Marek and sent him copies of the letters from the senators. It helped him feel like his voice was being heard. Marek sailed with that ship back over to Europe where he went home and married his love, Kate. A year later Marek and Kate had their first child, Monika. When I was in Poland in 1994 I packed a Barbie Doll in my bag to give to Monika. Unfortunately when I got to their home in Gdansk I found they were on holiday. I was able to give the doll to Marek's father with a note saying I was sorry I missed them.

Throughout the years we have exchanged Christmas and Easter cards and letters and photos of our families.

Marek and Kate had their second child, a son in 2000. In 2006 I had the blessing of going back to Poland and again, I missed visiting Marek and his family. That brings us back to Friday, March 12, 2010. "Captain" Marek is master of a container ship which happened to call in at the Bayport Container Terminal in LaPorte, Texas. Chaplain Lacy Largent from the Houston International Seafarers Center had duty on those docks that day. When Captain Marek asked her if she had my phone number she did one better. She called me and gave him the phone.

Captain Marek and Me

After our initial "happy to hear your voice" greetings he asked if I could visit his ship. Because of the new security measures I can no longer visit a ship in Houston on my own. Thanks to Chaplain Lacy, though, after twenty years of not seeing my friend, Marek, I was able to meet Lacy at the guard gate and have her escort me to the ship. She left me on board to visit while she finished her day's work.

Marek and I had a great time catching up, looking at family photos and remembering that day in February 1990 when we first met. I am so proud of him and all he's accomplished! The last time I saw him he was a fear-filled young man. The person I saw on his ship in Bayport is a confident, strong captain, husband, and father…a grown man! What an absolute joy! I love this vocation!

IN MEMORY OF NANCY

Tom is a long-time seafarer from the U.K. He is an avid reader and so whenever his ship comes into port he emails and asks me to bring him a box of books. His vessel works in the Gulf of Mexico and comes into Galveston to take on provisions or conduct crew changes every so often. I saw Tom in June of 2010 when he joined the ship after being on vacation for a few months. He was very busy the day I delivered the books. I asked him how his holiday was at home. He briefly answered that his sister died. He didn't have time to talk and so I could barely offer my condolences.

The ship went out to work on the Gulf and about six weeks later came back into port. Tom emailed and asked for more books. When I arrived on the docks with the books he came down the gangway carrying the previous box of books to exchange. He said he had gangway duty so he couldn't invite me in for tea. I asked if I could visit with him on deck. He said, "Of course you can!"

Our conversation began simply with Tom telling me provisions were being delivered the next morning and then they'd be sailing. I asked him how he was doing and he began to pour himself out. Six weeks prior he needed to do the same but was too busy to talk. This day, though, Tom let all the emotion out that he had held inside.

He told me about his sister, Nancy. She was a nurse and all her life she took care of herself. She didn't smoke or drink and ate well. She cared for the sick and was a loving person. She lived simply, saved money for retirement and looked forward to turning sixty years old in March of 2010. In the U.K. a person gains many privileges when they turn sixty. One of the treasures she looked forward to was the coveted free bus pass.

A short time before her birthday Nancy began to have health problems. Tom's wife, Annette, went with her to the hospital. Nancy was diagnosed with ovarian cancer. She was angry and thought it very unfair. She was extremely disappointed that her plans for retirement were derailed.

Annette became Nancy's care giver while Tom was at sea. Tom returned home and stayed there to help her last few months. As he spoke about the cancer and how it robbed Nancy of her dreams his emotions surged. He said angrily, "You should have seen her! She looked so different at the end. It's a dreadful disease!" Then he went off the subject of Nancy briefly to talk about others (friends) in his life he lost to cancer. One was a seafarer friend who had to leave the sea. He still needed an income so he chose to drive a taxi. One day while driving a fare, his friend dropped dead. The man had to climb over the front seat to pull the hand brake and stop the vehicle.

Eventually Tom's thoughts came back to Nancy. He said following her death the solicitor notified him and Annette that Nancy had left everything to them except for a few charitable bequeaths. Nancy never married and had no children. She saved money well in anticipation for her retirement. She had a house and furnishings. Tom looked at me and said, "I don't want her house. I don't want her money. I want her!"

His love for his sister was deeply apparent. They were good friends as well as siblings. They lived near each other and visited often. His love for her was as a brother's love should be for his sister; beautiful.

I sat listening to Tom on the hot deck for over an hour. He was emotionally exhausted when he finished. He apologized for talking so much. I told him it was a blessing for me to listen and learn about Nancy. I look forward to my next visit with Tom.

MEETING LAARNI: TWENTY-TWO YEARS IN THE MAKING!

In 1991, I was still serving in the Apostleship of the Sea, Port of Detroit, Michigan. I received a phone call from a ship agent one day alerting me to the arrival of one of his vessels in our port. They sailed from Cleveland. It was while the ship was in Cleveland that a terrible accident took place in which a young Filipino seafarer named, Jimmy, died. Upon arrival in Detroit I visited the ship and began grief counseling with the officers and crew. It was then that one of the officers gave me the name and address of Jimmy's wife in the Philippines.

Immediately I sent Laarni, Jimmy's wife, a Mass card to pray for Jimmy's soul and a letter of condolences. She wrote back sending me a photo of Jimmy, their daughters, Jennifer and Jaime Joy, and herself. I kept that photo in my office for years until Hurricane Ike destroyed all my records and photos in 2008. Laarni and I kept in contact through snail mail for many years. Then there was a time period when I stopped hearing from her but I continued to send Christmas and Easter cards and a letter once in a while.

Then, in 2013, I received a phone call from Laarni saying she had emigrated to the United States and was first living in California but just recently took a nursing job in San Antonio, Texas! She returned to the Philippines for a visit with her parents and they handed her a pile of cards and letters from me. She was overwhelmed that I never forgot her or the kids.

Laarni and Me

On September 7, 2013, I received a text from Laarni stating that she would be in Galveston with some friends for the weekend and was hoping to meet. I drove to Galveston's west end early on the morning of September 9 and there, for the first time in 22 years, Laarni and I met. We had a great visit catching up on our kids' lives and what Laarni is doing in San Antonio. It was such a nice feeling to finally meet this woman whom I walked with in her grief for a very long time!

Soon after our meeting I received a beautiful card from her daughter, Jaime Joy who lives in California. The very next day I received another beautiful card and care package from her daughter, Jennifer, who lives in Hawaii. In her note she wrote that on the day that her Mom and I met she had a dream about her Dad. It was so vivid that she woke up crying.

When she woke up she saw the photo of her Mom and me sent via text by Laarni. She said it felt as if her Dad was letting her know he was still always around and watching over them and that there are people in the world who still care about them as well.

The Seafarers Center may not be open 24/7 but the ministry continues at all times and sometimes for years and years and years!

Padre Sergio and I finished the third pear. The lesson was *love;* unconditional love; agape love. Sitting outside the church with the sun warming me, the sweetness of the pears curbing my hunger, and the refreshing water quenching my thirst I felt loved. God is love and He is here with us.

4

Fourth Pear - Peace

The next pear came out of the bag. Padre Sergio cut a piece and handed it to me. He smiled and said, "*Peace* is what we find in this pear. Peace is the work of justice. It is not sitting back and doing nothing. It is anything but inaction. Peace is very much a part of respect and dignity and love. You, my sister, as a Franciscan, are learning to be a bearer of peace. Inner peace radiates to those around you. Giving out peace brings peace back to you."

BORIS AND ANDREJ

On November 27, 1995, I received word from the Coast Guard that a Russian vessel reported an accident resulting in the death of a seafarer. I called the ship agent to get the details. Boris, the seafarer who died, was from Novorossiysk, Russia.

He was fifty-six years old, married and had two children in the university.

The ship, the M/V KAPITAN SPIVAK, was due in port November 30. Boris' body was brought to Galveston by launch on November 28. When the ship arrived I went on board and spent time with the captain and several crewmembers. The crew was grieving, but besides coping with the loss of a friend and the trauma of recovering his body after the fall into the ship's hold, there was the knowledge of knowing his family wouldn't receive any death benefits. "Since Perestroika," said the captain, "the company cannot afford it." It was touching to see the crew trying to collect money for Boris' family amongst themselves.

The next morning I visited the ship again. They were expecting to make a crew change at their next port in Israel. The Captain and Chief Engineer planned a personal visit to Boris' family to give them the money they collected. I was able to hand the Captain an envelope with US$340 to add to the collection from caring people in Galveston.

I spent a lot of time on board over the several days they were in port. I prayed they wouldn't go to anchor over the weekend since Galveston was hosting its pre-Christmas festival, "Dickens on the Strand." The festival would give them the opportunity to be welcomed into our community and have a relaxing two days rest. Two days at anchor would give them no relief from their grief. The news came late on Friday afternoon that they would be staying in port.

A second event took place within those two days. The captain, Edward, was baptized into the Russian Orthodox

Church with the chief engineer, Alexy serving as his godfather. The captain now proudly displayed a small silver icon he received from the pastor of the Greek Orthodox Church in Houston. Other crewmen began wearing their crucifix chains on the outside of their shirts rather than hidden inside. And on Monday evening, December 4, the M/V KAPITAN SPIVAK was blessed. Boris' death had a great effect on all of these men.

The third officer, Andrej, stood watch with Boris. Every time I visited the vessel, Andrej was present. There was one opportunity to talk privately in the mess with Andrej. Boris' death affected him deeply, causing great homesickness and longing to see his own family. We talked a long time.

The next morning I visited and some crew members wanted to go ashore. They asked to go to the store. Andrej was among them, but when it came time to get out of the van with the others Andrej stayed behind and asked to go back to the Seafarers Center with me.

At the Center Andrej recalled Boris' accident and spoke about his friend in great detail. He said Boris was kindhearted and gentle. Andrej himself was thirty-two years old, married and had a two year old son. Boris' death brought mortality into focus. At that time we closed the Center between 2 and 5pm, then we would reopen for the evening. When it was time to close the Center in the afternoon, Andrej asked if he could stay with me and see what my family life was like beyond my work in the port.

Andrej came with me to the high school to pick up my daughter and then to the elementary school to pick up my sons. He came home with us and we talked all while I cooked dinner. After dinner it was time for Andrej to return to his ship for duty. He was feeling much more at peace by that time. He came to realize that we must all face death someday but it is how we live that really matters.

The ship stayed in port several days and any time we work so intensely with a crew it is hard to say good-bye. At 6:00pm on Tuesday, December 5, I went out to pier 32 in time to see their lines being thrown. It was dusk and their faces were shadowed. As the crew members realized I was on the pier, more came over to the starboard side to wave and shout messages. Instead of a sad moment it turned out to be quite a fun sight.

Alexandre was on the third deck, waving both arms and bouncing up and down. Igor and Vladimir were on the main deck yelling, "Da Svidania, Karina!" and "Happy New Year!" Someone radioed the bridge and Captain Edward came outside, called down to me and waved. As the ship moved away from the pier there was Andrej, a silhouette in the grayness, silently waving a full arm wave from the stern. And then they were gone. I know I may never meet them again but there are days when they cross my mind and I whisper a little prayer for them.

DEL MONTE PLANTER

The reefer vessel DEL MONTE PLANTER called in the Port of Galveston every Sunday over Monday for most of 1996. During that time the Filipino crew became familiar with me visiting their ship. Weekly visits open opportunities for many kinds of discussions including shipboard prayer communities and lay ministry. The seafarers, most of whom were Catholic, came to know that I am a Catholic Ecclesial Lay Minister and that lay ministry within the Church was alive and well. I frequently held prayer services on board their ship and soon began to teach them that they could do this as well when they were not in port. On June 16 of that year the shipboard prayer community of the DEL MONTE PLANTER was born.

Del Monte Planter Crew, mission volunteer Bobbi Salaz, and Me

The first prayer leader appointed by crewmembers was a seafarer named Mark Jose. In the age of longer contracts and less time in port ships' crews find themselves not only far from home for a long time but far from their Church communities as well. Recognizing that they shared a community on board their ship they understood they could come together in community to pray. The seafarers talked about it and decided to have rotating prayer leaders so that when any of them signed off to go home the group would be able to continue.

There are many shipboard prayer communities started by chaplains all over the world. As land based prayer communities we need to be praying for their success.

M/V LAVENT-K

The bulk vessel LAVENT- K came alongside July 31, 1996 to load grain. I visited early in the morning and found the captain and chief officer quite busy. It appeared a mistake was made in the information they were given as to how long they had to load. This miscalculation in time caught them with full ballast tanks. Outside auxiliary pumps had to be brought in, so shore leaves were either severely shortened or cancelled altogether and tensions were mounting.

The ship had arrived in Galveston nearly a month earlier and had been anchored off shore waiting its turn at the grain elevator. All on board were from Romania and Turkey and were looking forward to a night in town. The captain had his taste buds all set for a lobster dinner at a nice restaurant. That wasn't going to happen now.

Seeing the frustration and disappointment in all the faces I asked the captain how I could help him to calm the crew. After a few seconds of thought he asked if I would be willing to take some of the crew to the Seafarers Center to call home then another group two hours later. That took care of about half the crew. The others had to be on board for the pumping and loading.

So between trips to the Center I spent time on board talking with others. It's amazing how calm they became by giving them time to talk about their disappointment and frustration. Eventually the subject changed from them not being able to go ashore to family and home. By the time they left they were feeling less angry and focused on their work. They would, hopefully, be able to go ashore in their next port.

M/V NIMET PISAK

Who would have guessed that when the ship NIMET PISAK came to Galveston they'd catch a Beatles (next generation) concert, enjoy time with children, and learn some origami?

Every evening for the five days the NIMET PISAK was in port, crew members came to the Seafarers Center to call home, relax, mail letters, but especially to see the children. My children, Angie, Danny and Anthony, happened to be the same ages of children of several of the Turkish crew. One of the seafarers in particular, Fuat, saw traits of his own son in Anthony. It was not uncommon to see Fuat watching Anthony fold pieces of paper into birds or watching Danny and Anthony play cards. Fuat played table tennis with the boys and watched TV together with all three children. And the seafarers who were present the night the kids' put on a Beatles' concert were truly entertained.

Spending time with our family at the Seafarers Center those few nights gave the Turkish crew much joy. And sharing my family with them gave me much joy. In

November 2010 I received a phone call from our port chaplain in Lake Charles, Louisiana, Deacon Patrick Lapoint. He said he had someone at his Center who wanted to speak to me. The next thing I heard was a voice I hadn't heard in years, "Hello, Sister! Do you remember me? I am Fuat!" What fun! Fuat and I spoke for a while and caught up on family and life. He asked about my children by name, remembering them well from his visit many years before. It was great to hear from him again.

CHRISTOS

In March of 1997 I boarded a ship at the sugar pier and was greeted on deck by some seafarers from Ecuador, El Salvador, and Nicaragua. I entered the mess and was greeted by some smiling faces in the galley.

The chief cook, Christos, a Greek seafarer, offered me a cup of coffee, he didn't know why, he was busy. But he brought it and sat down. And we began to talk about many things, mostly the life of a seafarer. Christos said he didn't know why he was talking so much. He was busy, though, and asked me to return at noon if possible.

I did return at noon and, although, Christos was getting lunch out for everyone, we continued our conversation. He had recently lost his father while Christos was sea.

After lunch he showed me pictures of his wife and sons. He told me about being at sea when both his sons were born. "Every time my family needs me, I am away, just like every time I need Jesus, He is far away." I asked him what he meant and he didn't know exactly why he said that. By the end of our conversation that afternoon, Christos and I knew he was in Galveston for a reason but we just didn't know why yet.

That evening Christos and some of his shipmates came to the Seafarers Center. They had letters to mail and phone calls home to make. There were many seafarers from other ships too. The Center was bustling with activity. Amid everything, I noticed Christos emerging from the phone booth obviously shaken. I went quickly over to him and asked him what happened.

His wife told him that his 16 year old nephew had been in a car accident and was in a coma. He is the only child of Christos' sister. He was experiencing feelings of disbelief, shock, desperation, and helplessness. He didn't feel like talking and went back to the ship.

The next day I visited the ship to check on him. He recalled our conversation about him being away from home whenever his family needed him the most. Then he said, "*Jesus is so far away, Karen.*" He was hurting badly. Unfortunately the provisions came and he had to supervise the process and we couldn't talk.

I went back to my office and sat quietly thinking about what he said. Then I wrote him a letter. I asked God to guide my hand to say the words Christos needed to hear. The letter turned out to be six pages long.

That evening, when I went to the ship to pick up the crew, Christos came too. I gave him the letter. He put it in his pocket. At the Center he called home again. The news was the same. He was deeply saddened because he had prayed his wife would tell him his nephew was alive and alert and well. Instead she told him only the machines were keeping him alive. Christos asked to go back to the ship.

Very early the next morning I visited the ship to see how he was doing. He was surprised to see me and he looked much better. He told me he read my letter. In it I told him that Jesus was near him always. That during the times he is in pain and his family is suffering Jesus was holding them and helping them carry the pain. I believed God knew of his nephew's accident and that Christos would find out when he called home. I believed God knew he needed to be somewhere where he would be with "family" for comfort. I was his "family" while he was with us. Christos felt that here.

He told me that after he read my letter he went down on the pier to use the phone to call his sister. She was at the hospital but he spoke with his brother-in-law. They had a long talk and Christos understood there was nothing he could do but pray. He returned to the ship and read my letter two more times before he fell asleep. He felt at peace.

PETROS

In 1997 on my visit to a Greek flagged bulk cargo ship, I met Petros, a 47 year old radio officer. He was anxious to talk with me. He had many things weighing him down. As ships became more efficient, satellite communications were making radio officer jobs obsolete. Within a year or two from my visit with Petros there would be no jobs for radio officers on ships. So a career move was evident for him.

He had been struggling with his future for over a year.

The Greek Seaman's Union offered to retrain radio officers as 2nd officers. It would mean more schooling and a more physical job. Many radio officers were between forty and sixty years old. The decision to be retrained as a 2nd officer was a difficult one. The alternative was not so attractive either. Leaving the sea and trying to find a job on land would not be easy.

So Petros often found himself wondering what he would do. Many times he spoke with his mother, who died in a few years prior to my visit. He said, "Momma, help me!" And he found comfort in that intercession prayer.

Petros was not married at the time of our visit but wanted to find a wife and have children to continue his family line. This desire coupled with his career changed caused much pressure to press on his mind.

Petros did not find any definitive answers while he was with us but he did find he could talk out his problems and in that, find peace.

RAUHL

In 1994, a ship came to Galveston which was manned by seafarers from Morocco. While they were in port I visited the ship and cared for the crew, helping them contact their families back home, getting them to the Seafarers Center to relax and have some fun, and just sitting and talking with them getting to know them.

It was three years later when I received a letter from Rauhl, one of the Moroccans on board. After leaving Galveston he had begun to think about Christianity. He began asking for Christian reading materials from port chaplains in other ports. It was late 1997 that Rauhl told me in a letter he was thinking seriously about becoming a Christian. He was very concerned, though, because Morocco is a Muslim nation and converting to Christianity is a dangerous act. He asked my advice about it. I was able to give Rauhl the name and address of a Catholic priest in Morocco who would help him through the process including advice on surviving as a Christian in a Muslim nation.

Sewing the seeds does not have to be complicated, forceful or even deliberate. By living the gospel we can, through our actions, lead others to Christ. "And they'll know we are Christian by our love."

JIMMY

On February 14, 1998, while the research vessel, SEABULK VERITAS was working in the Gulf of Mexico, a tragic accident occurred. Jimmy, a twenty year old seafarer from the Dallas, Texas area was on the aft deck when a nylon rope snapped severing his left arm and sending him over board into the sea. A shipmate saved Jimmy and pulled him back on board. Officers and crew worked to stop his bleeding and kept him calm for the three hours they waited for the Coast Guard helicopter to make it out to them.

Incredibly Jimmy's Mom, Debbie, was also on board as part of the galley crew. She was in the galley at the time of the accident. At Jimmy's request, Debbie was kept away from her son as he lay on the deck waiting for the helicopter. Unknown to him, Debbie ran up to the bridge and watched the activity as the crew cared for him and as he was lifted by basket into the helicopter.

Debbie had to wait until the ship sailed into Galveston to see her son at the hospital. Normally the trip could be made in fifteen hours but they had engine trouble and Debbie had a torturous thirty-six hours to wait. She was so afraid they weren't telling her the whole truth about Jimmy's condition and until she received a shore to ship telephone call from Jimmy on the 15th of February, she wasn't sure he was even still alive.

I visited Jimmy on the 15th after I heard about the accident on the news. His arm had been found and packed on ice but the long delay in getting him to the hospital made it impossible for the doctors to reattach it.

Jimmy's spirits were remarkable. He has a positive attitude and sees this as a new challenge, not a set back. His shipmates were traumatized by the incident and needed help with post traumatic stress. Many didn't want to talk to a counselor the company provided but drew strength from Jimmy's positive attitude.

Five days after the accident, Jimmy had surgery on his right hand, which had been broken in four places in the accident. The next day I visited and saw he was pretty much dependant on his Mom for eating, drinking, scratching, and pretty much everything except talking. His smile never faded. He was already trying to figure out how to do things for himself- and ways to get out of chores!

Jimmy was released from the hospital on February 20th and moved to a motel for a few more days of out patient care. A few days later Jimmy and Debbie went home. Since then he's gone through physical and occupational therapy all the while keeping his positive attitude. He is now married and has a family. Jimmy no longer works on the sea but he does work and support his family. Debbie keeps me informed of all the family news. And she loves being a grandma!

EDUARDO'S PAIN

On April 7, 1998, I received a letter from Eduardo, a Filipino seafarer whom I had been corresponding with for nearly eight years at that point. Eduardo's life has been a hard one to say the least.

I met Eduardo in October of 1990 when I was attending a course on seafarers' rights in New York. Eduardo and two of his shipmates were wrongfully discharged from their ship in the port of New York. This became a hands-on lesson in seafarers' rights for another student, Sue Helka, and me. We were able to help them and two of the three of them began corresponding and have continued over the years.

While on board another ship in 1993, Eduardo learned from his sister in a phone call home that his wife had abandoned their three small children to go to Japan to work as a dancer. Eduardo was devastated. His sister took care of the children while he was at sea. When he finished his contract he went home and became both mother and father to his children.

Eduardo tried very hard to give his children the love and attention they needed. In 1996 upon his return home from sea, he was met at the airport by his other sister. She had the sad duty of telling him that their sister who cared for his children died of a heart attack the month before. Again, Eduardo suffered deeply.

It was in 1997 that Eduardo's wife came back to ask forgiveness and attempt to reconcile. Eduardo felt his children needed a mother and worked very hard toward reconciling. We corresponded very much about it. He was happy his family was going to be whole again.

After many months of talking and counseling, Eduardo and his wife reunited the family. Eduardo returned to the sea to support them. Whenever he would call home to check on things, he would have to call his sister because he didn't have a phone at his house. She would give him the latest news. In late March of 1998, Eduardo called home and, again, was dealt a great blow. He was told that his wife had taken in a live-in boyfriend and one of his children had begged to come live with Eduardo's sister.

Eduardo immediately asked his captain to sign off at the next port, which was Hong Kong. Granted permission to leave the ship, Eduardo wrote me a letter, explaining the situation. He was completely distraught and lost. His mind raced with ideas to escape the pain. In essence his letter was that of a man who had lost hope. He was planning a murder, which was disturbing enough, but then he wrote,

Maybe in heaven there's total happiness, right? I'm waiting to what happens to me like Jesus said in the Bible, 'Come to me all you who are tired of carrying the heavy load and I will give you rest.' That is what I am waiting for.

I had in my hands words written by a desperate individual. It would take at least a week for a letter to reach him. That was no good. I needed some immediate contact with him. I began praying for him intensely and did so for twelve hours. I asked protection for him and his family while they worked things out. I knew he had no telephone, but prayed for an idea.

Over the years I kept records of hundreds of seafarers' addresses, including Eduardo's. I poured through my records and found a phone number that had been scratched out. I took a chance, said a prayer, and called the phone number. Wonderfully it was Eduardo's sister's home. When I explained who I was she knew me from my letters. "Oh, Sister Karen, Eduardo had a very big problem. He needs your help!" I explained I received his letter and knew he was very upset. I asked if he lived nearby so he could come to the phone. She said he lived nearer her sister-in-law and gave me that phone number. Then she called her sister-in-law and told them to run and get Eduardo for a telephone call.

In a little while I called the number. Eduardo answered and said, "Sister Karen is that you?" He was surprised I found him. I told him to go to the Apostleship of the Sea in Manila to see our chaplain, Fr. Savino. I told him Fr. Savino would be able to direct him to people who could help.

Eduardo went to the Apostleship of the Sea in Manila and got help. He began counseling shortly after and also got the necessary legal help to protect his children. I put Eduardo on my "Intensive Care" list immediately upon receiving his letter. That means I wrote to him daily, sometimes twice a day so that he could have an encouraging word in his hand every time the mail arrived. I also spoke with him in follow up calls to make sure he was doing better. It also means I prayed for him intensely.

Eduardo is a good man and a good father. I thank God he trusted me enough to write that letter.

M/V MLJET

When I saw the name of this ship as it came into sight in the Galveston ship channel I was excited. I had visited the MLJET several times when I was chaplain in the port of Detroit, Michigan seven years earlier.

In fact the last time I was on board in the early 1990s was during the height of the war in the former Yugoslavia. The MLJET was a Yugoslavian flagged ship at the time with officers and crew mostly from Dubrovnik, Croatia. Dubrovnik, at that time, was under attack. We desperately tried to get phone calls home through for the crew, but the phone lines were down in many places.

Then there was Steven. His call went through. Everyone gathered around him as he spoke to his wife, Mary. In the background he could hear the bombing- each time the explosions sounded nearer. Each time, Mary screamed in fear. Steven felt helpless wanting only to be there to protect her. Then the phone line went dead and Steven was screaming hysterically, "MARY! MY MARY! OH, MY MARY!"

We took him back to the ship and explained to the captain what happened. Steve was taken to his cabin by some of his shipmates and the captain promised to watch over him. I went to say good-bye to him and found him holding a photo of his wife to his heart. "This is my Mary," he said and gently kissed the picture.

As the ship left we kept them all in our prayers. We never heard of Mary's fate.

Fast forward to Galveston, 1998. As soon as the ship was cleared by Customs and Immigration I ran up the gangway and found the captain. After so many years I didn't expect to see any familiar faces and I didn't. The flag was now a Croatian flag and the officers and crew had changed over the years. I told Steven's story to the new captain. He understood my feelings about his ship. He had no knowledge of Steven or Mary, but spoke about that time and the effects it had on his own family and home.

Seeing the MLJET brought back some sad memories, but meeting new people and sharing those memories helped all of us. We still pray for Steven and Mary and all those who have suffered in similar ways.

In my living room at home I have a potted plant that always reminds me of the war in Yugoslavia. A Croatian seafarer gave me a cutting of a plant he had on his ship. It was the only thing left of his home after the war and he carries it with him wherever he goes. He cuts pieces off and gives it to people he meets in different ports around the world. He calls it the "plant of life" since it survived the war. He wants to keep it alive all over the world. It is a plant of peace.

DANNY

On an evening in September of 1998 the phone rang at the Seafarers Center. The seafarer on the other end of the line asked for me. It was Danny, an American seafarer I met five years earlier when his ship he docked in Galveston every 10 days for six months.

Back then, Danny was well into abusing alcohol and drugs, womanizing and getting himself and some of his shipmates into trouble. At one point another crew member was killed after many of them, including Danny went on a drinking binge in Mexico and the young man fell overboard and was swept away by the current.

Those were dark days in Danny's life. We had many long talks whenever I visited his ship. He knew he'd have to change his life or die but he wasn't ready to or strong enough to do it.

For a time after the ship changed routes and Danny signed off I kept in contact with him through letters but eventually we lost contact when he moved, leaving no forwarding address.

To hear his voice on the phone that night was a joy. And to hear his new ship was in Galveston after five years of not seeing him was a blessing. As Danny spoke and told me how he's been working hard to turn his life around that was the best news. He told me how he had been sober for several months and that he was making a conscious effort to repair relationships and make amends. He realized, during his dark years, that he could have died for many different reasons but God had other plans for his life.

That night Danny talked to me for two hours. He said most of the guys on the ship went into town for the night. He wasn't into that scene anymore and needed to call me to have someone to talk to. It was his way of staying safe- not getting talked into going ashore. He asked for a directory of Seafarers Centers so that wherever he went he could go where someone will care about him.

His ship was staying in port a few more days so we made a plan to meet at the Seafarers Center the next day. Danny came into the Center that night and the smile on his face told all. It was so good to see him and so good to see him healthy. He talked for three hours, I listened. It was important for him to tell me the details of the last five years including his suicidal thoughts and plan. He had since sold the gun he stared at the night he wanted to die. At the end of the evening he thanked me for having faith in him and never giving up that he would find his way. I continue to keep Danny in my prayers.

LECH AND ANDREJ

In October of 1998 the Catholic High School where my children attended held its homecoming game and festivities. Homecoming is an American high school tradition during the autumn. It happens during the football season at a game played on the "home" field of the school.

Each class, grade 9-12, designs and builds a float (which is usually a flat bed trailer or truck decorated to a certain theme.) Also the student body votes to make two senior (12th grade) students the King and Queen of homecoming. There are special pre-game festivities, half-time festivities including the crowning of the King and Queen, and usually a homecoming dance follows the football game.

This particular year, two spectators at the O'Connell Catholic High School homecoming game experienced an American football game for the first time. Lech, chief cook, and Andrej, a fitter from the ship SMITWOJZ SINGAPORE came to the game with my family and me. Both seafarers are from Poland and are European football (soccer) fans. But they thoroughly enjoyed watching the game. The O'Connell school colors are red and white (same as the Polish flag) so Lech and Andrej said they knew which team to cheer.

Cheerleaders were also a new experience for them. Often we heard them comment, "Very nice dancers!" They enjoyed the parents' excitement in the stands and laughed hard when a mother behind us began to lose her voice. Lech said, "Tomorrow her husband will be happy!"

Although O'Connell lost the game the seafarers saw two spectacular pass receptions and they said that was the best part of the evening.

M/V SMITWOJZ SINGAPORE RETURNS

I began teaching theology part time at the O'Connell Catholic High School in August 1998. Sometimes I shared ministry stories with the students. They knew I brought Lech and Andrej to the homecoming game that fall. So when it came time to make up Christmas boxes for the Seafarers Center I asked my classes if they would like to participate and they did. Twenty-five Christmas boxes were made up from students in my theology class that year.

On a Sunday in November some of my students came to the Seafarers Center for a tour and then a tour of the port. It was then we discovered a wonderful surprise. The **SMITWOJZ SINGAPORE** was back in port. Lech and Andrej were still on board. The students were able to deliver their gifts to the whole crew and see their appreciation. Andrej gave them a tour of the ship and Lech brought out some treats from the galley. It was great fun.

PRAY FOR ME!

A young Filipino seafarer who was a cadet when I visited the Philippines for the first time in 1997 was sailing on his first ship in 1998. Being far from home, he was lonely and needed to hear from family often. When I met the cadets in Cebu, Philippines the year before, I spoke to them about my correspondence ministry. They each wrote down my address and were eager to write and tell me about their first ship experience.

Through the correspondence ministry I learned about their trials and tribulations as new seafarers. I heard their excitement over new places they visited. They shared stories of making it through storms, seasickness, and interactions with other seafarers. And they loved to tell me about their visits to Seafarers Centers around the world.

One day a letter arrived from the cadet I mentioned at the beginning. It was a very disturbing letter. In it he wrote:

Dear Ate Karen,
   Hello, how are you? I just received your letter today. Thank

you very, very much for keeping in touch. We are here in Slovenia about a kilometer from Italy. We just came from South Africa and we are going to Norfolk again then Hamburg.

We had heavy work today. We just take out our main engine piston. We start at 6am and finish at midnight! About our situation here, we have a good team in the engine room but our captain is not very well. He is always drunk. Just last night he was mistaken to find our ship because he came from ashore and he went to another ship. The chief officer of the other ship told us that our captain crawled up their gangway and demanded to stop the loading! He was very drunk. He don't know where his ship is!

Ate, please pray for me!

I wrote him back right away, "*Yes, Little Brother, I pray for you and for all who go down to the sea in ships. May God keep you safe and well and return you safely to your family.*"

I then called the Center for Seafarers' Rights in New York to report the drunken captain and alerted our port chaplain in Norfolk, VA to have the Coast Guard standing by for when they arrived.

M/V VIOLETTA

On the morning of December 28, 1998, at the entrance of the Galveston Ship Channel, fire broke out in the engine room aboard the M/V VIOLETTA. Seafarers began fighting the fire that soon raged out of control. The captain gave the abandon ship order and as the crew assembled and were accounted for, they found two missing. Emmanouil, the chief engineer and Nikitas, the 3rd engineer were not among the others. The captain and several others went back to look for them. Their search was hampered by heavy smoke. They couldn't enter the super structure let alone get to the engine room where the two were last seen.

The captain made the painful decision to continue to abandon ship. He wanted to stay and continue to search, but the Coast Guard forced him off as well. The ship burned for nearly two days. Special fire fighting teams were brought in to contain the blaze before the diesel fuel ignited. Late on the second day the bodies of the two men were found.

I began working with the crew as soon as I received my first call from the Coast Guard. I took clothing and Christmas boxes filled with personal toiletry items that they would certainly need since they lost everything in the fire. They were taken to a local motel where they would remain throughout the investigation.

Violette Crew and Me in St. Patrick's Church in Galveston

The captain, Gregorios, and the two men who died were Greek. The chief officer was Serbian. The twenty-two others were Filipino. The captain and chief officer were extremely busy with the Coast Guard inquiry and meetings with ship owners' attorneys, company representatives, and Cyprus flag officials. I held regular meetings with the crew to write down their questions and concerns to try and get the answers.

The first day our Seafarers Center provided them with phone cards to call home. Because of the two deaths, the news of the fire was being reported internationally and their families were worried. I sent an email to each port chaplain in the Philippines with a list of crew families so they could provide pastoral care for them. When one crew member, Romulo, called home he was told his wife collapsed when she heard the news of the fire on the TV and was taken to the hospital. He was sick with worry. I contacted Fr. Roland Doriol at the Cebu Seafarers Center and he went to the hospital to visit Romulo's wife. Later he sent me information to relay to Romulo via email.

The families of the two Greek seafarers who died were visited by company representatives and their priests. The chief officer said his family was okay and there was no need for us to find someone in his home town for pastoral care.

On December 31 we held a Memorial Communion Service for Emmanouil and Nikitas in our Center's chapel. During the service we talked about the dangers and difficulties of life at sea. We talked about always staying near God as we never know when it will be our turn to be called home. And we talked about the beauty of the sea and how God is in those moments of serenity and peace.

I held two roses and spoke about their beauty but how they die and that is that. But when we die our beauty; our souls live on. It is the part of ourselves that is most precious and needs the most care. After everyone received communion and silently reflected on why we were gathered, a seafarer walked to the altar and kissed the feet of Jesus on the crucifix. It was a very reverent moment.

For two weeks after the fire the investigation kept the seafarers of the VIOLETTA in Galveston. The company paid their stay at the motel and had them eat on an account at a restaurant nearby. Unfortunately that restaurant had no rice on the menu. Since rice is a main staple of the Philippine diet, having none posed a problem. After a few days of eating french fries rather than rice, the Filipinos were feeling ill. So I began cooking rice, lots of rice – and taking it to the motel for the crew. They were so happy to have rice again. This was a daily delivery for the remainder of their stay.

Finally, I was able to spend time with Captain Gregorios after a week of no contact at all. The Captain was grieving the loss of his officers. He had only met Nikitas when he recently joined the vessel and it was their first time working together. Still it was a great loss. Emmanouil and Captain Gregorios, on the other hand, had sailed together for ten years. They were neighbors at home and both had two children who were friends. Captain Gregorios lost his best friend.

During the inquiry I had no access to him, but one day I

made my way through the Coast Guard personnel, attorneys, and company representatives and gave him my card. He said he saw me helping the crew all week and appreciated it. I told him any time he wanted to talk I'd make time to listen. Immediately he stood up and led me out of the room. In the next room, he offered me a chair and sat opposite me in another. He said, "I am so alone. They don't know what is inside of me." And he talked for two hours! After that, every time I went to visit the crew I made time for Captain Gregorios too. It was his "safe" place to cry, to be angry, to fear, to let himself be vulnerable.

On January 6, the chief officer, 2nd engineer and two oilers were taken back to the burned shell of the VIOLETTA that had been towed into port. At the request of the seafarers I went too, as it was going to be very difficult for them. But it was necessary for the investigation.

All of us had to be outfitted in hazardous materials suits, including a respirator mask, to go inside the ship. Again, at the request of the seafarers, I went in first with Coast Guard personnel to bless the ship and all those who would enter the vessel for purposes of investigation. We prayed for the souls of Emmanouil and Nikitas at the place where their bodies were found. We prayed for strength for those who survived to get through this difficult time and for all their families.

The crew then re-enacted their actions during the moments of crisis for the investigators. It was a long and extremely dangerous ordeal. Later, when it was over, I spent time with the seafarers who went in that day to let them talk it out. It was very traumatic.

On Saturday, January 9, all but Captain Gregorios were released from the investigation and sent home. I spent several hours with them all saying our good-byes. Captain Gregorios was scheduled to leave the following evening. That gave us more time to talk. I gave him a cross with a guardian angel on it. He was happy for the gift.

He spoke a long time about his family. He is proud of his children and how they have grown up. He looked forward to seeing them soon. He was so weary from the events of the past two weeks.

Captain Gregorios told me that before they left for the airport the youngest Filipino seafarer came to him and said, "Captain I do not understand how these people (Seafarers Center staff) could care so much for us and not ask us for any money. Why do they do that?" Captain Gregorios answered him, "That is what the Seafarers Centers are for. To help us when we are most desperate for help and no one else sees that. Always remember the Seafarers Centers when you are in port and most especially when you need help."

When it came time to say good-bye to Captain Gregorios it was difficult. I knew the Filipinos would be cared for by the port chaplains back home, the chief officer seemed like he was doing okay, but Captain Gregorios was hurting badly. He was going to need on-going pastoral care so I asked him for his address. He wasn't home long before a letter arrived from me. He answered:

Dear Karen,

With great relief I got your letter and I like to express you my thanks for your kindness and interest for my life...Also I will like to assure you that my thoughts are in Galveston and I cannot forget the tragedy that happened...

My flight back home was easy and now with my family try to recover from all that happened to me and forget but it is not easy. I must thank you also that I am always in your prayers and I will like to ask you to always pray for the two of my friends who passed away.

Please you not forget me and be sure that always I shall waiting to hear from you.

With best wishes to my God sister,
Gregorios

In March I received a letter from Captain Gregorios. The pain suffered on the VIOLETTA increased. He wrote:

My dear Karen, before get a little better from my own suffer and pain and before reach to place myself psychological under better control we have lost on February 4 my wife's brother from a heavy stroke in the age of 55. You understand how big pain now in the whole family....his name Dimitris.

Understand such circumstances my dear Karen (Adelphi) my life and my problems as you may understand are quite enough...and must fight always.

I received your card and letters and the GANGWAY newspaper and my crew's photos...and I said to myself that one beautiful soul some where in this world is very close to me and worry about me....I want to tell you that this give me strength and hope together with my family I am sure that I will pass all these memories that gives me so much pain.

I continued writing Captain Gregorios letters of encouragement and hope, reminding him of his faith in Jesus. In April he wrote:

Up to date my life it was one continuous battle for surviving in the jungle of various problems and difficulties till I met you under the tragedy circumstances that already you know....That moment when you came in my life up to now you have pass to me the light of your spirit, the kindness of your heart and nice words which you had to believe give me the picture of another world. It is imperative beautiful to me to hear from you, read your letters full of hope, faith and peace.

I received all your letters and Easter card which I read almost every day and I take from them strength, faith and hope that another day will rise tomorrow for me and my family.

Captain Grigorios' wife, Christine also wrote expressing her grief over the loss of her brother, Dimitris. Her pain was deep and also watching her husband suffer so much from the VIOLETTA tragedy was very difficult for her.

Over the years we continue to correspond. Captain Gregorios has not gone back to sea. He was so deeply affected by the VIOLETTA tragedy that he gave up the sea and treasures being with his family.

ARTURO

During the time of the crisis of the VIOLETTA, I visited other ships in port. On one of the vessels I encountered Arturo, a Filipino seafarer who pleaded, "PLEASE HELP ME!" Like many Filipino seafarers, Arturo signed a 12 month contract. He was well into his 14th month when I met him. He was promised to be repatriated from Veracruz but that didn't happen. Again he was promised to be repatriated from Galveston but upon arrival he was told he'd have to wait until the ship crossed the Atlantic and docked in Egypt!

On Christmas Eve, Arturo received a telex on board saying to call home immediately. When he called home, his family told him his father died. Arturo is the only son and requested immediate repatriation to help his mother and sisters in this tragedy. Again the company said no.

Arturo pleaded with me to help him when I visited the ship that day. Immediately I called the Center for Seafarers Rights in New York and requested their aid. I faxed a copy of Arturo's contract and the telex about his father's death. The Center for Seafarers Rights attorney faxed the company in Greece on his behalf requesting immediate repatriation pointing out the terms of his contract and his special circumstances regarding his father's death. Within 24 hours the captain received a telex from the company approving Arturo's repatriation.

I was on board at 7am the next morning to monitor the situation. I witnessed Arturo being paid off what was owed him, signing off and leaving the ship to be transported to the airport. Arturo was extremely grateful. Sometimes we are their only voice.

TEDDY

On one of my visits to the ships in June of 1999, I met a chief engineer from Poland named Teddy. We had a polite conversation about Poland and the U.S. and a little while later Teddy told me about his son.

Teddy has several children. His son, Janusz, is his youngest. He was seventeen at the time of my visit. Teddy called home and received news that Janusz did not pass his class due to excessive absences from skipping school. Teddy began to blame himself for not being there.

I explained in 1998, I had the opportunity to start teaching part time at the Catholic High School in Galveston. I told him that I saw students from two- parent families fall into trouble as well as students from single parent families. We discussed that, although Teddy's absence may have been a factor in his son's behavior, there were other influences as well. Blaming himself was not going to help his son.

Teddy's ship was due to leave that evening. We would have no time to continue the conversation on this trip. I went back to the Seafarers Center and wrote him a letter reinforcing the things we discussed and encouraged him to have hope. Enclosed in the envelope I placed a special prayer for teenagers through the intercession of St. Gerard. Teddy and his family are Catholic so he understands intercession prayers.

When I finished my night duty that evening, I went to the

ship and left the letter on Teddy's desk in his office. I hoped it would be a nice surprise when he came up from the engine room to do some paperwork.

MEETING IOAN AGAIN

Ioan and I have been friends since his ship came into the port of Detroit in 1990. In 1990, aboard his ship, the M/V LEO M, we had trained an Extraordinary Minister of the Eucharist (EME). The EME led the communion services at sea. Ioan, an Orthodox Christian from Romania, noticed a change in his shipmates. He said he never felt the same love among a crew since.

Ioan and I have corresponded since that time. We have been through a lot together. Ioan is a Chief Engineer. He tried desperately for years to help his family immigrate to South Africa. His hopes of that have faded. In December of 1996 Ioan wrote:

Long time I was quiet. I received your letters. Thank you very much. Now I am again on board a ship for a new contract. The name is AGIOS VASSILIOS and in one way it looks like the LEO M. Be sure I will never forget your kindliness. To have the chance to talk with somebody who understands and knows the seaman's life give me strength to surpass some hard period of this life. I wish you and your family much happiness and a Merry Christmas!

He is married with two daughters. When Ioan lost his mother a few years after we met we corresponded through his grief and pain. His family is everything to him and when he is at sea he misses them very much. In February of 1997 he wrote:

> *I send you many greetings from South Korea. The life goes on and I am again on sea. I spoke on telephone with my daughter. Everything is okay (in my daughter's opinion!) How are you? How is your family? The time is passing and I don't know how long I will stay on the sea. God be with us.*

In November of 1999, I went to Houston to visit the travelling ITF museum ship. It was while I was there that Houston Port Chaplain, Rev. Ben Stewart, told me a ship was in port on which there was a Romanian seafarer who knew me. I asked him the name of the ship and he said, "ALABAMA RAINBOW". Immediately I knew it was Ioan because I wrote him letters on that ship!

It was eight years since I saw him and, not wanting to miss the precious opportunity to see him, I asked for directions to the ship. About twenty minutes later I was at the grain elevator in Houston. Once on board I asked the young seafarer on watch to call the chief engineer and tell him his sister was here. In a flash, Ioan came running up from the engine room saying, "I knew it was you!" Others came into the mess room where he took me when they heard the commotion. Ioan explained to them who I was when my letters arrived so they all knew me. His friend, George, the electrician on the ship, was smiling broadly, "He is very happy you are here."

Ioan fixed me a cup of tea and we began our long awaited visit. He kept repeating, "Eight years!" I couldn't stay for more than an hour because it was late and I had to drive home to Galveston but we both agreed the visit was worth it even if we only had a short time.

WITALI

I met Witali and other members of his crew while I was in Davao, Philippines in November 2000. I was there with other colleagues to attend the dedication of the new Stella Maris Seafarers Center in Davao. One afternoon we went to Paradise Island by boat to relax and enjoy the day. While others cooled off in the water I was reading under a tree. I heard some people speaking Polish nearby so I wandered over to their picnic table and asked them what ship they were from. Surprised to see a non-Filipino on the beach they asked me to join them. I thanked them in Polish and we became instant friends. We spent the afternoon talking about their families and their ship route. They were telling jokes and it was really a fun time.

Once I was home from the trip I wrote them a letter thanking them for a very nice afternoon, and sent it to the Stella Maris Seafarers Center in Davao. My friends at the Stella Maris delivered it to the crew when they came back into port before they changed routes. I received this reply from Witali:

Karen!

A few days ago I came back home via Greece. After I met

you in Davao, Philippines we go to Tokyo and then Korea. Inchon was last port in that area. Afterwards two months we sailing to South America across Pacific Ocean to bananas loading in port, Porto Bolivar, Ecuador. From Ecuador we go to Greece, Turkey and Egypt. After discharging cargo vessel come back to Greece when all crew members disembarked and come home to Poland. Thanks for your letters. Happy Easter to you and your family.

Your friend,
Witali

It was a simple afternoon relaxing on the beach in the Philippines. It was just a little window of time but a happy memory.

UNCLE JOHN

As the season began Christmas gifts began to arrive at the Seafarers Center from all over Southeast Texas. We began delivering them aboard ships that would be at sea for the holidays. Countless smiles were given to us in return. The gifts help the seafarers feel part of the community.

We were blessed that year (2000) to have three ships' crews with us on Sunday, December 17 for our annual Christmas Party at the Center. Seafarers from the M/V ALAM VERACRUZ, the M/V PETROMAYA, and the M/V CREDA representing the countries of the Philippines, Indonesia, Croatia, Panama, Guatemala, Honduras, and Mexico enjoyed a turkey dinner and a visit from Santa Claus. Guests from many area churches and our Seafarers Center staff and families were on hand to make the festivities bright with caroling led by West Isle Presbyterian Church's organist, Ms. Drew Taylor. Everyone agreed it was a great party.

The Christmas gifts were coming in faster than we could deliver them at one point. Little by little, though, gifts were delivered to grateful seafarers. Ernie Bright, our Center manager at the time, and I were touched by the reaction of some Bulgarian seafarers who simply could not believe the gifts were for them. Through teary eyes and choked throats they thanked us over and over again.

On the third day of Christmas I took Christmas gifts out to the oil rig, "UNCLE JOHN". They came into Galveston in December for the past several years. The captain told me that as they were heading to Galveston knowing they would dock after December 25th the crew asked if he thought if the Seafarers Center would still have gifts for them. Last year they received their gift delivery before Christmas. That year the captain told them they would have to wait until Christmas morning to open their gifts. The gifts were all placed under the Christmas tree in the mess room. The seafarers were very anxious and on Christmas morning around 3:30am the captain received a phone call in his cabin asking, "Can we open them now, Captain?" He said they were like excited little children.

As we unloaded the 64 gifts necessary for the UNCLE JOHN crew I could see the excitement again. The crew piled up the gifts into the basket that is hoisted up by a crane to the platform. Once all the boxes were ready the captain radioed the crane operator with a simple message, "Take her up, Santa!" Then he turned to me and said, "You people don't know what these gifts mean to them; to us. Thank you."

M/V HYDRA

In February 2001, I visited the M/V HYDRA. On board there was an inspection taking place so all were busy. I promised to return later in the evening to give them a ride into town.

That evening the Seafarers Center was filled with seafarers from Turkey, Bulgaria, and Romania. They were full of life and enjoyed the time ashore. When it came time to take them back to their ship I quietly loaded some of the last of our Christmas boxes into the back of the van. When we got to the pier I opened the back of the van and asked them to help me unload the gifts. They were very surprised to see the brightly wrapped presents being that it was February. I explained that the people in Southeast Texas were extremely generous this year. Their faces were beaming as they carried the gifts up the gangway.

They were in port a few more days and spent each evening at the Seafarers Center. On the evening they were scheduled to leave I went out to the docks to watch them throw the lines and pull away from the pier. Many of the seafarers stood on the deck waving and, as busy as he was, the Bulgarian chief engineer, Gencho, ran up on deck briefly to wave good-bye as well. He shouted, "Thank you, sister!"

With the fourth pear finished I thought about the lesson on peace. I search for peace constantly in my life. I want to bring peace to others and know I cannot do that without first having it within my own heart. Padre Sergio and I sat quietly for a while. The birds were singing. Peace was around us.

5

Fifth Pear - Serenity

The day was hot and the pears tasted very good. The water was refreshing. I could hardly wait for the next lesson. Another pear came out of the bag. As I bit into the slice Padre Sergio began to speak, "*Serenity* is very closely related to peace and has an element of surrender to God's will. Life is hard, sister. I do not have to tell you that. We both have faced hardships and joys- sometimes all in the same day. You taught me that as we walk along our path we come across others who are suffering or stumble into something that causes our own suffering and yet, God is always with us. Sometimes we walk along our path and come across someone who just needs to share some time on our path. God is there too."

BIG MAC ATTACK

Anyone who works in a Seafarers Center, at least in the

United States, knows the frequency of requests for a ride to Wal-Mart is high. Raising a family while working as a port chaplain can get tricky at times, but most days I was able to cook dinner for my children before it was time to work the night duty shift at the Center. One night, though, that wasn't the case. So when I had a request to take some seafarers to Wal-Mart, my kids came along for the ride. The plan was to get the kids something to eat while the seafarers shopped. There was a McDonald's restaurant inside the Wal-Mart, so that's where we decided to have dinner.

While we were sitting down, two of the Russian seafarers we brought shopping wandered into the McDonalds. They had never been in a McDonalds before, although they had heard of them. They also heard the name, "Big Mac" so that is what they ordered.

When they received the "Big Mac" boxes they joined my family at our table. When they opened the boxes, Victor said, "What is this?" Both began to explore their sandwiches by removing the top bun and looking under the patties. They rebuilt the stack and tried picking it up. "How do you eat it?" was another question. The kids giggled as the two finally got the hang of it and attacked their "Big Mac" just like everyone else. In no time at all they were seasoned fast food specialists.

RICZARD

On the morning of January 26, 1996, I boarded a bulk cargo ship. I spoke with a Filipino seafarer in the mess. He told me there were Greek officers, Filipino crew and one

Russian electrician. My visit with the young man gave me no indication of concern.

In the passageway I met a seafarer whom I thought must have been the Russian because his face was neither Filipino nor Greek. I greeted him in Russian and he said, "Not Russian. Polish!" I was surprised because the mess man did not mention a Polish seafarer on board.

I asked him, in Polish, how he was and at that point a door opened and yet another Polish seafarer emerged. Soon I was surrounded by Polish seafarers. And believe me, they all wanted to talk! Apparently the last leg of their voyage had been a rough one. Not the water for the seas were calm. The on board tensions were high. The Polish and Filipino seafarers got into a fight at their last port in Brazil. Two Polish seafarers ended up in the hospital with stab wounds. The Filipinos were not charged by the Brazilian police because they said it was a ship matter.

If that wasn't bad enough, while underway, the chief officer from Greece fell into the hold and had to be air lifted by a Coast Guard helicopter to a hospital in Mobile, Alabama. The chief engineer, also from Greece, suffered a chemical burn on his face and in his eyes shortly before they docked in Galveston. I met him as he waited for transportation to the hospital.

It was interesting how the situations affected the seafarers differently. As we progressed through this somber discussion one of the Polish seafarers decided that they had been too stressed for too long. Riczard slid into a slap stick routine that would have given Dick Van Dyke a run for his money. At first the others thought he was crazy but when he wouldn't let up they began to laugh. Once the ice was broken, the stress poured out. Marek, the youngest of the six Poles, had been sitting on the floor. He fell over laughing, and tears streamed down the faces of all of us. All of Riczard's jokes were in Polish, but his actions were universal. I needed no translation. No one would have guessed that five minutes before we all sat together with serious faces and somber moods.

When all was calm again, there were smiles and a peace in the room. They found their way to cope and they knew they would be okay.

NURTURING FAITH

Sometimes as port chaplains, we get caught up in the everyday kind of needs of the seafarers. We bring them telephone cards to call home, provide them with transportation for shopping, make sure they have internet service or cell phones on board. It can be very easy at times to be anything but spiritual with seafarers.

I find it extremely important to keep an open heart out on the docks. That is when the Holy Spirit begins to move and make God's presence known. Meeting a seafarer such as Jerome from St. Vincent can be an ordinary experience until the Holy Spirit enters making it an extraordinary experience.

Visiting on board his vessel I spoke with many seafarers. Requests for rides to the Seafarers Center or shopping seemed to be the majority of requests. As I made the plan for evening pick ups Jerome came over to talk with me. He saw I was wearing a crucifix and asked me about it. He is Christian but felt alone on the ship. The others were Christian as well, but none of them felt like openly expressing their faith. Jerome wanted badly to have a shipboard prayer group. Since no one else was interested, he felt very sad. I made sure I had his ship's address before they left and he also gave me his home address asking me to write to his wife.

I wrote him right away so that the letter would catch up to the ship in the next port or as soon as possible. He received my letter and wrote back:

Sis, I was very glad to hear from you and to know I have someone like you to keep me up with kind words. And when I look at this wonderful picture of Jesus it makes me feel so happy....this picture you sent means a lot to me. Did you write my wife in St. Vincent yet? I tell her about you and she was glad to have my sister give Christian love to all at home...

I did write to Jerome's wife and we exchanged several letters. She told me about the prayer groups she was involved in and that she wished Jerome could be involved in a prayer group on board as well. We take for granted our freedom to practice our faith in our community. A shipboard community does not always welcome those who want to practice their faith. When a small prayer group does form aboard a ship it becomes a beautiful flower blossoming.

THE LOUSIANA

The LOUISIANA was a Liberian flagged oil platform in for some conversion work at the Pelican Island dry dock facility. There were about 50 people on board working in twelve hours shifts around the clock. There were workers from the U.S., Scotland, Mexico, Poland, the Philippines, and Brazil. Many were on short three week contracts but the Poles and Filipinos were on six month contracts, which consisted of twelve hour days, seven days a week, getting one half day off per month.

On a schedule like that, it is difficult to find time to come ashore or even relax and get rest. But at least once a week we got a call at the Seafarers Center for a pick up at the LOUISIANA. The Polish and Filipino seafarers mailed their letters home, bought personal toiletry items and phone cards, played a little table tennis, and walked around the city a bit.

I knew they were unable to come ashore to go to Mass either Saturday evenings or Sunday mornings, so I offered to bring them Holy Communion and have a service, being that they were all Catholic. They gained permission from the captain, who gave me clearance with dock security to come aboard and so on November 14, 1997, I boarded my first off shore oil rig to come together with all those who wanted to pray.

At the service we prayed for their families, their safety, and their commitment to God. I spoke to them about their special circumstance of being on board with a demanding schedule. The time we spent together in prayer was warm and friendly. And we shared in Communion with Jesus. What a blessing.

My anxieties over climbing what I was told, over sixty-five feet to get on board were quickly eliminated by the smiles and prayers of those on board. So the climb down was not so bad. It went so well that we had another Communion service for Christmas singing hymns in English and Polish. It was great joy sharing our faith in such unusual circumstances.

HENRYK

I received a call from a ship agent who told me that a Polish seafarer had been brought by Coast Guard helicopter to our hospital in Galveston. He was suffering from a possible heart attack. When I arrived at the hospital, I found Henryk hooked up to monitors and resting. I introduced myself and told him I'd visit him as long as he was in the hospital.

At that time, Henryk was 31 years old. He was working on a ship in the Gulf of Mexico when he began to have severe chest pains. His father died of a massive heart attack at age 46 so Henryk was worried. As the pain increased he went to the captain and asked for help then fell ill on the bridge. The captain called the medical officer to the bridge and Henryk was given morphine as the US Coast Guard was called for help. About five hours later, Henryk finally found himself in the hospital.

Doctors ran many tests and Henryk was told his heart was fine. More tests were ordered to find the source of his pain. A few days later Henryk was told that he has a stomach ulcer. He was so relieved it wasn't his heart! We had long talks about many things during his stay in the hospital. Every time I walked in, Henryk gave me a big smile.

On the night before he was discharged I blessed him in Polish. He was so touched by this, he couldn't speak but mouthed the words, "Thank you." The next day Henryk was sent home to Poland to rest and recover.

CAPTAIN ANTE

This is a story of a man who was searching for answers to questions that had no answers. Captain Ante came to Galveston on a liner vessel, a ship that has a regular run from one port to another so we see the crew often. Captain Ante is from Croatia. At this time he was a young captain, but far from inexperienced. He had already experienced things like saving his crew in a monster storm in the Atlantic to nearly dying of malaria in the Middle East. Over the years he proved his seamanship and wisdom time and again.

I met Captain Ante when he first came to Galveston and got to know him as he returned often. On one visit he had a disagreement with his chief mate. Although he was correct to fire his chief mate, he was feeling badly about it. He knew the man had a family, but the captain must maintain discipline on board. The day I spent on board listening to Captain Ante vent about the incident he kept thinking about the man's family. Finally he threw his hands up and said, "Why didn't HE think of his family?"

As our visits continued over the weeks, he confided in me his silent pain. He and his wife had been married 15 years and have two children. His wife has been chronically ill for many years. He has taken her to doctors and specialists and no one can find anything wrong. He was beginning to think she was less physically ill and more mentally ill. He was slipping into despair.

We had the opportunity to have Captain Ante's ship here on several Sundays. He is Catholic but hadn't been to church in a while. I invited him to go with my family one Sunday. After thinking about it, he decided to go.

At Mass he sat with us and was surprised to see the laity participating as lectors and Extraordinary Ministers of the Eucharist. In his country, the old ways were still prevalent. He liked what he saw and the way he felt. He came with us to Mass four times over the months his ship came into port. On one of my visits he said, "My wife will be so surprised when I come home and say, 'Let's go to church!'"

In our conversations he also told me about his relationship with his parents being strained for the past fifteen years because they opposed his marriage. He was hurt by the things his parents said to him about his wife. He financially supports his parents because his job allows him to do so, but his parents only praise his brother.

Captain Ante and I had several months of visits to talk things out and put things into perspective. We exchanged emails and letters when his ship wasn't in port. I tried to give him things to think about and offer encouragement. In an email one morning when they were in port he wrote:

Dear Sister,

I read your letters just now. Thank you very much for the letters of support. It's very nice feeling that somebody – you– understand me and try to help, showing me the right way. I wait for your visit today.

Capt. Ante

When it came time for Captain Ante to go home in early December 1999, he was excited and longing to see his family. He decided he would invite his parents and brother's family to his home for Christmas in hopes of reconciliation. He was anxious most of all to be with his small children again. He missed them so much.

Over the years Captain Ante and I have kept in touch via email. His ship has only come back into port once since that December.

ROOM ANN

In June of 1998, a staff member from the Seafarers Center in Freeport, Texas called to say a crew member from the M/V HARBEL CUTLASS had been taken to our hospital in Galveston after falling into the ship's hold. Expecting the worst from the thirty-five foot fall, I hurried to the hospital where I found Room Ann, the Taiwanese bosun in the Intensive Care Unit awaiting surgery. He was alert and smiled when I told him I was from the Seafarers Center in Galveston.

Room Ann had two children at that time: a girl, age fifteen, and a boy, age eleven. He was at the end of his contact and would have been signing off to go home from Freeport. He was a seafarer for several years, then found a land job to stay near his family but was economically forced to go back to sea this trip.

Room Ann was taken for surgery that day. He was in the recovery room when I returned the next morning. He had his right pelvic region repaired and would undergo another operation in a day or two.

Room Ann was moved to the orthopedic floor following his surgeries. He was anxious for the arrival of his wife. The company had agreed to bring her to Galveston to help him in his recovery. He was very upset that his bag of clothes was missing when he returned from surgery. He was told to take off his wedding ring for the surgery, so it, too, was in the missing bag.

He called me at the Seafarers Center, distraught over losing his wedding ring. He hadn't slept all night and was very stressed knowing his wife was coming soon. I went to the hospital security and asked for assistance in locating Room Ann's possessions. Within 15 minutes of showing up with security, Room Ann's bag was returned to him. He dug into it, searching for his ring, and pulled it out with a great big smile. Then he broke down crying and thanking me for helping him.

Room Ann wanted to talk about the accident. He said he was checking the holds to make sure they were clean. He leaned over to check the ridge and lost his footing, plunging headfirst into the hold. He remembers trying to grab onto anything he could- but he was falling too fast and only badly bruised his arm on a ladder rung. His attempt to grab the ladder was enough to turn him so when he hit the bottom his head and back were not injured. I asked him if he knew about God's angels. He thought a moment and then smiled brightly, "Yes, angels!" he said.

Room Ann's wife, Coni, arrived five days after his accident.

Room Ann was moved to a room in the rehabilitation part of the hospital. Coni learned to help him in and out of his wheel chair and went to his physical therapy with him every day.

At the beginning of July, Room Ann and Coni left Galveston to return home to Taiwan. Room Ann was expected to recover fully. He felt very fortunate to have this second chance.

MACARIO

I met Macario in February of 1996 when his ship, the M/V ANNA L, came to Galveston. He was having some problems and we were able to help him. He has kept in touch through correspondence since.

In 1998, Marcario set aside his seafaring career temporarily to take the job in Taiwan. He wrote and told me he was in Taiwan so when Room Ann was released from the hospital in Galveston and sent home, I sent Macario a letter telling him about Room Ann and gave him his address in Taipei. Macario knows too well the hazards and suffering involved in a seafarer's life.

After consulting a Taiwanese friend about Room Ann's address he realized Room Ann and his family lived quite a distance from where Marcario worked. He'd have to use an entire day off to travel there. Determined to be a "brother" to someone in need Macario and his Taiwanese friend set out to find Room Ann. Happily, they met and Macario wrote later to tell me of their meeting and how Room Ann and Coni were amazed that someone who knew their "sister" Karen in Galveston worked in Taiwan and came to visit. I also received a letter from Room Ann and Coni thanking me for the surprise visit from Macario and thought of it as another "angel moment."

TIGER

I visited a Chinese bulk ship one morning in 1998. On board I met a young seafarer who has a wonderful smile. Right away he wanted to talk and ask many question and practice his English. He wasn't a maritime cadet. He simply joined the ship to work. He was curious about the world and was full of life.

While the ship was in port I visited often to continue our conversations. When I asked him his name he answered in Chinese. He explained in English that it meant 'Tiger', so he told all his friends to call him Tiger. Tiger and his shipmates came to the Seafarers Center each evening. They played table tennis, phoned home and, on one occasion, I helped Tiger fill out a post card for his girlfriend.

Tiger and I exchanged addresses and corresponded for a few months while he was still at sea. During those letter exchanges, Tiger became curious about God and asked many questions. I did my best to answer him and give him food for thought. In his letters he expressed a wish to be able to find work on shore when he returned to China. Life at sea was adventurous and fun, but only for a short time. He loved his country and wanted to be there. A life at sea would keep him far away for too long.

In September of 1998, his ship arrived in Shengzhen. Tiger

signed off and went back home for a vacation. After a month with his family and friends he wrote:

Sister,

After a month's rest I came to Guangzhou. I found a job in a Canada Computer Company. I work as a salesman now. I like this job. It is very exciting because I can interface with many different people and it can improve my ability. I hope that God can help me do this job well.

Do you remember my girlfriend? When I was in Galveston you help me write a card to her. She is very good and even more beautiful than before. May I ask you to add her name to your daily prayers? She will graduate next year.

How is your family? My family is very good. I have four elder brothers and one elder sister. The third and fourth elder brothers are still in the University for the Master's degree. The eldest brother have a family and lead a peace life. The sister is married and have a lovely baby.

Karen, you are in my heart. I hope you have a happy life with your family. God be with the earth.

Everyday I pray for you,
   Tiger

That was the first time he mentioned he had so many siblings! I was amazed because I know that the law in China is one child per family. So I had to ask him how his parents were able to have so many children. His answer came back that they had the children before the law changed. He thought they were a very "blessed" family.

MELCHIOR

Sitting down for a cup of tea with Chief Officer, Melchior was an experience. Melchior, named for one of the Magi, is a Croatian seafarer. He had been sailing for 25 years when I met him in 1998.

Melchior was born and raised on a Croatian island. He is married and has a son and daughter. He spoke about his country and the war that took place there in the early 1990s. He spoke about the destruction and rebuilding, the escapes and refugees. He has a deep love for Croatia.

As our visit progressed, Melchior spoke about life as a seafarer and recounted an experience of his ship sinking in the Persian Gulf. His vessel went down due to a missile attack in the middle of the night. He said he always knows God is with him, but that night was the only time he ever called out to God saying, "Okay God! I know you are there. I REALLY NEED YOU RIGHT NOW!" He and all his shipmates were saved.

Melchior is Catholic. He said, "All of Croatia is Catholic." He is not a very religious man but knows God is with him. He keeps God in mind.

He spoke about life at sea and life as a family man. It is difficult. He is gone many months then comes home. But instead of relaxing, he often has a list of repairs to make at the house and other responsibilities waiting for him. And if he sees something his children are doing that he doesn't like- in particular staying out late, he cannot say anything. His wife set the rules and he cannot change them for the months he is home, which he said is very frustrating.

But when all is said and done, Melchior's best moments in life are when he could experience another sunrise or sunset – be it on the bridge of the ship or on his front porch at home.

M/V WILD COSMOS

Tuesday evenings in the summer are a Galveston tradition. For nearly 100 years, the Galveston Beach Band has played music in the park to the delight of residence and visitors to the island. One Tuesday evening in June of 1999, a few Indian seafarers from the WILD COSMOS, a regular reefer ship bringing bananas into the port of Galveston, attended their first Tuesday night concert in the park.

At that time, Tuesday nights were my nights' off and I often took my children to the park to listen to the Beach Band. While ship visiting earlier that day, I mentioned the concert and asked the seafarers if they would like to go. They did, and so it was a family outing for all of us.

One of the traditions of the evening is to ask people in the audience how far they came to attend. When the seafarers proudly proclaimed they were from India, they were given a prize for travelling the farthest.

The enjoyment continued with popcorn and snow cones and the great kids' parade, where all the little children in the audience parade around the park behind the American flag while the band played, "The Mickey Mouse Club Theme".

The seafarers, missing their own families, were very happy

to see the small children dancing and playing in the park. They asked to go to the concert again when their ship returned. We made it a regular practice throughout that summer.

BRIAN

When I first arrived in Galveston in 1992, the Apostleship of the Sea World Congress was being held in Houston. That is where I first met Brian. He was a maritime cadet and part of the Philippine delegation. Throughout the Congress I got to know Brian and we kept in touch afterwards. He graduated and began to sail. I only have a few excerpts from his letters that survived Hurricane Ike but I'd like to share them with you.

In January of 1996 he wrote from Cebu, Philippines:

Dear Ate Karen,

I got hold of your letters and I am very glad to have received them. Thanks a lot once again– you know, my brother and sister, my cousins appreciate very much your loving concern for seafarers. They've asked how you manage to find time writing us.

I've seen my seaman brother, now in Leyte. It's great to be once again together with our parents. We took together the third mate license examination last January 15-17. We don't know yet the result. Hopefully next week.

That's all for now, Ate. Please help pray for my cousin's safe delivery of her baby. God bless you and good luck for everything you do.

I remain in prayer,
   Brian

Brian passed his exam and became a third officer. He always wrote to tell me when he was boarding a ship again and made sure I had the address of the shipping company so I could write him. While he was on board a ship named BLUE HAWK in late 1996 he was slightly injured when the ship was undergoing a US Coast Guard inspection in the Port of Baltimore, MD. He was hit by the lifeboat crank and was injured on the right side of his face. He wrote to tell me about the accident and not to worry. He received proper medical care and was able to sail with the ship.

I saw Brian again when I went to the Philippines for the Apostleship of the Sea World Congress in the Philippines in 1997. He was doing well and moving up in rank. The last time I saw him was when I was in the Philippines in 2000 for a Crisis Management Training seminar. He came to see me because he was on vacation from the sea and just took the exam for his master's license. My little brother, Brian became Captain Brian! It was very exciting to be there for this event.

SHARING BIRTHDAYS

A ship came into port in March, 2001 to load grain. The seafarers on board were mostly from Vladivostok, Russia and a few from Romania. They were in port once before a few months earlier and received Christmas gifts from our Seafarers Center. When I boarded the ship this time, they were all thanking me for the beautiful gifts they received. The 3rd officer said, "Everyone was so happy!"

Andrej, the chief cook, heard I was on deck so he came out from the galley and invited me to lunch, thanking me for the gift he received at Christmas. I spent lunch time with the crew and enjoyed Andrej's cooking. Later that evening they came to the Seafarers Center to make phone calls home and relax.

Andrej saw the table of used clothes and the sign that said, "FREE". His eyes lit up as he went through the pile and found white shirts he could use in the galley.

The next morning I went to the ship again. I found they were nearly loaded and preparing to leave within two hours. Wandering into the galley after greeting the busy deck crew, I found Andrej not looking very happy. He was preparing lunch.

He offered me tea, and despite his broken English and my broken Russian, we had a good conversation. Andrej said that it was his birthday and also the birthday of his twin sister. He was sad not to be with her on their special day. It also happened to be my birthday that day, so when I told him his whole demeanor changed. He did have his sister to celebrate with him on his birthday! All of a sudden I was holding a ham sandwich and getting a big hug from my new "twin brother". He somehow whipped up a small pastry to share with me. He was truly happy.

God has shown me time and again that we are all somehow connected. Sharing Andrej's birthday with him was a great birthday present for me, too.

PLANTING SEEDS

I met Vladimir, a Bulgarian seafarer, in 2001. I visited the ship on which he was working as it loaded grain bound for Europe. At coffee time, Vladimir came into the mess. He asked me where I was from and I told him the Seafarers Center. Vladimir immediately proclaimed, "I am an atheist." I said, "I just see a good person." He gave me a curious look and then sat down.

I asked him about his homeland and family. He began to tell me about Bulgaria and the beauty of the mountains. He said he loved going to the mountains when he went home for vacation. They were peaceful.

We didn't talk about God that first meeting. Vladimir knows I am Christian from the crucifix I wear. He also saw the time I spent with Victor, his shipmate, whose brother just had surgery to remove a brain tumor.

Vladimir wanted to talk again each time I came on board. One visit he wanted to talk about religious fanatics. The ship was in port four days and we had some long conversations. When it was time for them to leave Vladimir and I exchanged addresses to continue the conversation.

Vladimir and I have been corresponding since then. He always signs his letters, *Your atheist friend.* But the content of his letters continue to be curious and subtle questions about God. In a letter written in July of 2004 he enclosed a copy of a *Reader's Digest* article he came across entitled, "Searching for the Divine." (March 2002) His letter simply said, "*I hope this will be of interest to you.*" I read it and wrote him back, commenting on the article. In a previous letter he said he went to an Orthodox Church with his fiancé` and was quick to add, *"to make her happy."*

Following Hurricane Ike, when Vladimir heard I lost everything in my office including his letters and the photos of the mountains he sent me, he sent again photos of the mountains, wild flowers, sunsets, etc.; the places where he finds peace and serenity. He promised to write again too.

In his first letter following the hurricane, he wrote and told me that he was married in Brazil to a woman named Maria, a Roman Catholic. He said they are very happy. He said he loves Brazil and the nature there is beautiful. He asked me to pray for them because his ship was sailing in pirate territory. And he signed it, *"Your friend,"* not *"Your atheist friend."*

His next letter was in early 2010. He wrote:

Dear Karen,

Thank you for your letter. I am glad that you not forget me. And I am really happy with Maria, my wife. I stay two times in Brasil, three months each time. Still not speak well Portuguese, but I understand many things. For me Brasil is fantastic country.

I am happy that your Seafarers Center is open again. I hope no more hurricanes come to Galveston.

What else for me. After Singapore my ship go to Brasil, but I don't know the port yet. I hope to see Maria again. And after about two and half months back to Singapore for crew change. Five crew members will be signing off to go home, but with this volcano (in

Iceland) is impossible. I hope when come my time no volcano, no hurricanes, and other things.

You tell me before that I have a (guardian) angel that cares for me. Now I start to the read the Bible. Very interesting. You know that I am atheist and read Bible to be ready to argue with someone. What you say about this....Genesis, Chapter 1:26, 'And God said, let us make man in our image, after our likeness." Strange! Ah! You know me very well. I like to argue but you take this easy. I hope I am your friend. If you write me soon I will receive your letter when I go back to Singapore.

...I am thinking again about the Catholic Church. For some priest is prohibited to married, for some (ministers) like you is okay to marry. Not fair.

Thank you for your letter. I hope you write me again soon. Sorry for my English.

Your friend,
Vladimir

Whenever I receive a letter from Vladimir I answer him right away. I can tell he is anxious to hear what I have to say. This is what I wrote back to him:

Dear Vladimir,

Hello, friend. It is very nice to hear from you. Your English is much better than my Bulgarian! Thank you for writing. And now you are learning Portuguese! That is wonderful.

All is well here. Our Seafarers Center is still under construction but it is looking better and better. We are only open *from 9:00am to 5:00pm until our new doors and windows are installed. Today begins the construction on the windows! This is good news.*

*I know you are an atheist, Vladimir. That was the first thing you told me when we met. I respect your beliefs. I like that you are reading the Bible and the verse you chose to argue, Genesis 1:26 is a good one. Let me help you understand the **"us and our"** in that passage. We, Christians believe that the words "us" and "our" refer to the Trinity: Father, Son and Holy Spirit. One God but three persons. Saint Patrick explained the Trinity to children by telling them it is like the shamrock. Three parts but all one leaf.*

There are many things in faith that are strange and hard to understand. But faith is about trusting. In the book of Hebrews 11:1 it says: To have faith is to be sure of the things we cannot see." I cannot see the angels that care for us but I am certain they are there. I have many stories of angels I will share with you in future letters.

I want you to know that your angel asks me to pray for you. So I stop my work and pray for you. The prayers are for grace and peace.

God bless you, Vladimir. I look forward to your next letter.

Your friend,

Karen

Vladimir continues to search. He continues to communicate. I continue to answer his questions, plant some seeds, and water them with prayer.

AN AMERICAN SHIP

In February of 2000, while I was making ship visits, I boarded an American flagged bulk ship and made my way to the Captain's Office. Usually I stop by the galley first to pop in and say hi, but that day something told me to go right up to the Captain's Office. As I approached, I saw one of our local U.S. Coast Guardsmen in the office and I heard him say, "Well, we have a port chaplain here…" I stepped into the doorway and he said, "Here she is now!" Then looking toward me he added, "Chaplain, we were just talking about you."

Behind the desk sat the captain and standing next to him was a ship's surveyor. The surveyor said, "She is probably non-denominational. I said WE NEED A CATHOLIC." When I said, "I am Catholic." He gasped and he said, "We need your help! You have to help us! They have demons in the engine room!" The Coast Guardsman looked at me skeptically and said, "It's all yours, Chaplain!" Then he got up and left.

The captain looked at me hopefully. The surveyor desperately begged me for help. I asked for details about what was happening. I asked if a person was possessed. He said no. If he had said yes, I would have called the Archdiocese for help from an exorcist priest.

The captain explained that their ship had just left Houston with a load of food aid for Bosnia. As they were coming down the ship channel, one of their fuel lines broke and the engine room was in danger of fire. A tanker ship was approaching them in the ship channel and suddenly the second fuel line broke, leaving them dead in the water.

Frantic about the fuel lines, possible fires, and a tanker fast approaching, everyone on board was terrified. Suddenly their engines started up and they were able to maneuver away from the tanker and come into the port of Galveston for repair. That in itself was impossible; there was no explanation for how the engines were able to start.

They had shore crews on board repairing the fuel lines. Every time they were close to being ready to sail, something in the engine room would fail. Repair after repair, break after break. The engineers were frightened and refused to go back into the engine room. They were ready to pack their bags and leave the ship when they surveyor suggested calling a Catholic chaplain. I agreed to help.

During my senior year at a Catholic high school, my theology teacher was an exorcist priest. In class he used to tell us stories of his exorcisms and how we must always guard against the devil. He also taught us how to pray in situations like this.

I told them to gather everyone into the mess while I went down to the van to get my prayer book and holy water. Back in the mess we gathered in a circle and prayed the Litany of the Precious Blood of Jesus and some simple exorcism prayers. Then I needed to go into the engine room and bless it with holy water. No one wanted to go with me. The surveyor said he would go and led me into the engine room. There we prayed for God's protection from evil and I blessed the engine room with the holy water. Suddenly a great peace swept through the area. The surveyor's eyes were very big and he said, "Did you feel that?" I smiled. He gave me a big hug and said, "You don't know what this means to us!"

The crew went back to work. They fixed the fuel lines and all the engine gauges. All was restored, the shore side workers and the surveyor left the ship, and the ship set sail for Bosnia via Wilmington, DE. A week later I received this email:

Karen,

Thank you so much for your efforts aboard the vessel…I want to give you a progress report of the ship after it's coast wise voyage to Wilmington. Yesterday afternoon the Chief Engineer called me to report that only minor problems were encountered on the trip over to the East Coast and that the ship's equipment and engines were working very good overall. Now that is a prime example of the power of prayer, and I thank you for delivering that prayer with such dignity and respect. Our God, indeed, is an awesome God."

Bob

AVE MARIA

In 1993, I met a Russian seafarer named Igor. His vessel came to Galveston every 10 days and we got to know all the crew well. After about six months this young seafarer said, "Karen I want to hear 'Ave Maria'." He knew I am Catholic. I was able to find a beautiful recording of Ave Maria and made a tape for him. He was so happy. Later, after Igor went home he sent us a photo of him and his wife at their wedding in a Russian Orthodox Church.

I was reminded of Igor when I visited a ship seven years later. Captain Sergei and his crew were with us four days. I visited daily and they came to the Seafarers Center nightly. On the last day in port Captain Sergei was excited to see me on board. The previous night he bought a CD player. He ushered me into his office and said, "Karen, I want you to hear this special CD." The music began. It was the Russian singer, Nikolay Baskov singing, "Ave Maria." Beautiful! What a joy to share that special song once again with one of my Russian brothers! And just like Igor's story, Captain Sergei made a tape of the song for me as a surprise. God's little blessings are wonderful!

Both recordings were lost in Hurricane Ike. Although the tapes are gone the memories live on.

IGNACIO

On a Sunday in February in 2001, after Mass at St. Patrick's Church in Galveston, I was approached by a fellow parishioner who volunteers at the hospital. She told me about an Indian seafarer who was there and was alone and scared. She couldn't remember his room, the floor number or his family name but she told me he was Indian and Catholic and his first name was Ignacio. She also said he was on the 5th, 6th or 7th floor.

I went to the hospital and began on the 5th floor. At the nurses station on the "A" wing I asked if they had a patient from India with the first name Ignacio. No. At the "B" wing I received the same answer. The "C" wing was the same but when I got to the "D" wing the nurse behind the desk smiled. I found him!

Ignacio was a young seafarer from Goa, India. Goa is a region in India that is primarily Catholic. The residents of that region often have Spanish surnames due to the influence of the Spanish missionaries. Ignacio was surprised he had a visitor. He worked in the galley department on our Carnival cruise ship, CELEBRATION. He was only 24 years old. This was his first ship.

Ignacio became ill on board spiking a high fever and his legs swelled. He was taken to the hospital for tests and treatment. He was never in a hospital before and, being far from home, he was scared.

I introduced myself and we talked a while. He told me about his fears and that he wished his family was there. I asked him if I could be his family while he was in the hospital and his smile and teary eyes gave me my answer. He needed some vital information from his hometown doctor so I provided him with a telephone card to call home. The information was given to his doctor here and his medication was adjusted accordingly.

I visited Ignacio daily brining him some reading material and a rosary. I visited the morning he was being discharged and taken back to the ship. He was worried he might not be well enough to work but said he would try. Ignacio stayed well enough to work out his contract.

PADME

On December 26, 2004, the strongest earthquake in over

forty years struck off the coast of Sumatra, Indonesia creating devastating tsunamis in the Indian Ocean. The death and destruction left in its wake was unimaginable.

As phenomenal efforts were being made to get desperately needed aid to the millions of victims, the mail was delivered to the Seafarers Center on December 30. Among the usual office mail was a late Christmas card for my family from a seafarer named Padme and his family. Holding the envelope, my hand began to shake. My heart began to race when I looked at the return address before opening the card. Padme was a seafarer from Sri Lanka, one of the hardest hit countries of the disaster.

My eyes teared up as I read the post mark- December 21, five days before the tsunami hit. Inside the card Padme wrote wishes for the New Year and signed it from him, his wife, Rangika and their child, Ranuga. I feared for them and began to pray.

Padme and I met 14 years earlier when I was still working in the Port of Detroit, Michigan. We kept in touch all those years via snail mail. I avoided thinking about Padme and his family when the news of the tsunami broke because it would be too painful. The arrival of his card forced me to think about them- again a reminder from God- it's not about me, it's about them.

I began prayer vigils for them. I asked friends to pray for them. I had restless nights wondering if they were okay. The second night after Padme's card arrived I had a nightmare where I was standing on high ground and they were on the beach playing with Ranuga. I saw the wave coming and screamed for them to take the child and run. They didn't hear me. I woke up filled with tears and could only pray.

After a week of agony I decided to write them a letter. If by some miracle they were safe and could still receive mail we may hear from them. Until then I had lifted them up to God. He knew where they were and what they needed. I trusted Him to see to their needs.

One month after sending my letter I received this reply:

Dear Karen,

Received your letter with many thanks. Myself, my immediate family members and most of my friends are safe. But still we don't know about some relatives and others.

My wife and child were at her mother's place for the holidays. That is about 100 miles to the center of the country. So on December 26th I was travelling to join them from Talangama, where we live. Also here live my mother and elder brother. My other brother and his family live about six miles away to the land side. Our house is about 10 to 12 miles from the sea.

That day I left home at about 8:30am and was travelling by bus. When we were passing the "Kelani Bridge" which is on the outer limits of Colombo we saw people crying and running saying the water current on the river had come up. We didn't take much notice about it. We thought it was due to recent heavy rains. Anyway, as the bus was travelling towards Karanegala town my brother rang my mobile phone and told me the situation.

My other brother who is in Germany will be coming soon

with German friend. They have collected money and will bring it here.

Once again thanks a lot for all your prayers and great concern about us.

Padme

What a great relief to hear from him. Knowing he was safe but his family and others needed help we were able to send our tsunami relief funds directly to Padme to help those around him.

EDWIN

One evening in January 2007, my cell phone rang. On the other end was Edwin, a Filipino cadet on board the M/V FILIA. He said, "Mom, can you bring me some food?" That can be an alarming question to a port chaplain. I said, "Is there no food on board? What's wrong?" I visited the ship earlier in the day and no one said there was a shortage of food. He confirmed it as well, "We have food." Now I was confused.

The crew of the FILIA had no US visas therefore no shore passes. They were grateful for the use of our cell phones to call home and I was running errands for them since they couldn't go ashore. Edwin asked again, "Mom, can you bring me some food?" I said, "Yes, what do you need?" Then he told me and I thought for sure I was not hearing him correctly. I asked him to repeat it. He did. Again I heard what I thought was, "Cheese curls." I said, "Cheese curls?" He said, "Yes, cheese curls." I still thought I wasn't hearing it right so I said, "Are you asking me for cheese curls?" He said, "Yes,

Mom, cheese curls." At that point I swore I was talking to one of my own kids. By then the conversation was so funny we both were laughing. Melissa Clarke, our manager at the Seafarers Center, overheard my side of the conversation and was laughing as well.

After hanging up, I told Melissa that it will be extremely embarrassing if I get all the way out to the ship with a bag of cheese curls and find out he wanted something completely different. I never had a seafarer request cheese curls before. So I went to the store, bought three big bags of cheese curls and drove out to the ship. I climbed the gangway with the cheese curls, filled out the security form, received my security badge and permission to enter the ship. In the crew's mess I found Edwin. I held the bags of cheese curls behind my back and said, "What did you ask me for?" He smiled and said, "Cheese curls, Mom." I produced the bags from behind my back and he jumped up and took them saying, "Oh thank you, Mom!" I love days like that.

Serenity. San Giovanni Rotondo is a beautiful area in Italy. The mountains, the fresh air, the holiness of Padre Pio's earthly home are, indeed, serene. I had no idea how many pears were in that bag that day. The lessons were rich and the pears were wonderfully refreshing.

6

Sixth Pear - Humility

The last pear came out of the bag. We were quiet for a while. We both knew it was the last pear in the bag. Padre Sergio sliced the pear and said, "*Humility.* All things, sister, are given to us by God. Our gifts, our talents, our blessings...all from Him! We must acknowledge this and keep ourselves from thinking we are who we are and where we are because of our own making. We are merely His instruments in the world. We work so that others may know Him through our actions, words, thoughts. As we finish this last pear let us remember this day, these lessons, and our God who is with us always."

THE SEAFARERS' CONTRIBUTION

The ship was one of many which came into the Port of Detroit in December, 1991. It was a liner vessel and we had taken care of the same crew every five weeks for the past two years.

The ship arrived at 5:30am that day. I boarded the vessel a few hours later and distributed the Christmas stockings my children made for the seafarers. The rest of the day was spent running some of the crew around town and getting ready for the Christmas party that was to take place that evening.

In those two years we had gotten to know the seafarers on this ship well. They had been to the home of one of our volunteer lay ministers and to our home several times over the years. They always sent letters or post cards whenever they were away.

On this evening twenty of the twenty-seven crew members came to the Seafarers' Center for a traditional turkey dinner. Good friends, good food, and good fun. Over half of the crew was Muslim, but they joined right in with the Christmas carols and some even danced to "Jingle Bells" with our volunteers. After dinner we gave them their Christmas gifts. Everyone had a great time.

The next morning I boarded the ship. On deck several of the crew gathered to give me letters to mail to their families, cancelled stamps from letters home for my children's stamp collection, and many thanks for the party. I watched them close the hold covers and get ready to leave.

The captain called me to his office and presented me with a large donation for our mission. He said it was a contribution from the ship owner in appreciation for all we had done for them. It was a very nice donation and I was grateful. As I was leaving a few of the Muslim crew from Maldives called me on the side and handed me US$23.56 as their donation. They gathered together that morning and pulled change and dollar bills from their pockets to give something to us for a gift, not because they were forced to do it but because they wanted to do it. They gave from their hearts.

To paraphrase Jesus in the gospel of Mark: "Amen, I say to you, these poor seafarers gave more than all other contributors to the mission. For the others have all contributed from their surplus wealth, but the crew, from their poverty, had contributed all they had, their whole livelihood."

And as I left the ship, the gangway was lifted, and the crew waved vigorously shouting, "Merry Christmas, sister!"

"MOMMA, PLEASE LISTEN"

Back in the 1990s we were still placing calls for seafarers. It was before the introduction of the phone card where they can just dial the toll free numbers and then a pin number to access the use of the card. Prior to that we had to place to call at the Seafarers Center and then receive time and charges from the operator following the call. One morning in 1996 I placed a call for a seafarer from Romania. He had been working six years on an off shore oil rig supply boat in Galveston.

The phone was ringing and he was anxious. He was calling his mother whom he hadn't seen in six years, but called whenever he could. The connection was made and his conversation began. Normally once the connection was made I took care of something else and gave the seafarer privacy. Less than a minute into his conversation, though, this seafarer was loudly saying, "Momma, please listen!" It caught my attention because he was so upset and he was speaking English.

When he was finished a few minutes later, he emerged from the phone booth in tears. I approached him and asked him if he was okay. He explained that being in America six years and speaking English everyday on the job he had forgotten many words in Romanian. His mother couldn't understand him as he spoke English mixed with Romanian. Out of frustration she said in Romanian, "You are not my son, I don't understand you anymore." His tears were streaming and his heart was heavy. He was a sad sight leaving the Center that day. He knew he was welcome to come in and talk if he needed to. Right then, though, he just needed to be alone.

CAPTAIN JURGEN

The stories I have heard as a port chaplain aboard ships and in the Seafarers Center are stories no one can invent. Real life can be far more interesting than fiction.

In 1996 I met a German captain aboard a reefer vessel bringing bananas to Galveston on a regular run. I met with Captain Jurgen each time his ship came into port. He was a very gracious man and I enjoyed visiting with him. Being very busy when the ship was in port, I could only occupy some of his time.

One day on my visit, Captain Jurgen told me the story of his own birth and survival in a postwar German town.

Seventy-five babies were born in his town that year, but only three survived their infancy. He was one of them.

Food was scarce in postwar Germany. Like others, mothers were malnourished. Therefore, infants could not survive on their mother's milk. The captain attributed his own survival to his grandfather who was a German soldier in the war captured by the British army. While he was imprisoned as a POW, he saved the bread he was given to eat, dried it, crumbled it, and sent it in letters home to his family. Captain Jurgen's mother took the bread crumbs and added some water to feed her infant son. This is how he survived.

Watching Captain Jurgen tell this story I could see the deep love he had for his grandfather and his genuine gratitude for having survived. Captain Jurgen knew I am Roman Catholic and watched how I cared for his crew and how I listened to him on my visits. This went on for several months. Shortly after his return home I received a letter from him telling me he had decided to become a Catholic and began taking classes at the local parish. He received the sacraments some months later.

Captain Jurgen and I have kept in contact over the years. He has since retired from the sea and enjoys a land based job near home.

On the same vessel there was a Croatian seafarer. Croatia is part of the former Yugoslavia. The war that had been raging in that region has changed the face of towns and villages. And the lives of the people will never be the same.

This seafarer heard the captain's story. He, too, had a friend, a fellow shipmate, who was born in postwar Europe.

Everyone in Europe call the children who were born and survived between the years 1945-1949, a "hearty breed," because of the difficulties families faced in those years.

This man's friend survived the hardships and overcame the odds only to find his fate in a bullet in his homeland's conflict nearly fifty years later.

In the mess room I met the new mess man, a young Filipino who barely looked eighteen. I asked him if this was his first ship. He said no, that he worked on a passenger vessel before.

He was happily washing the morning breakfast dishes as we talked. He used to wash the dishes for thousands of passengers and crew. This morning he was pleased with only twenty-five dishes!

He spoke about his time aboard the passenger ship. Passenger meal buffets were set up for breakfast, lunch, dinner, snacks, and midnights. He and the others working in his department were only able to get three hours sleep a day and sometimes they'd have to skip that too if a special buffet or dinner was arranged.

He spoke about the mountains of garbage produced by the passengers. He said there were days where he just couldn't take the smell any longer. And the crew was fed only the left over food from the passengers' buffets.

As he finished up the last dish he was happily moving on to his next chore without a complaint or regret.

The last story from this vessel comes from another Filipino seafarer waiting to be picked up to go to the airport. He was flying home three months short of the end of his contract.

He received a telex that his mother had died. By the time he received the news, requested to go home, and waited for his replacement to arrive, his mother had been buried for over a month. There was no need to hurry home for a funeral now, but he still needed to go home to visit her grave and be with his brothers and sisters.

The stories are real, the courage and pain is real. Our response to listen and show care and concern must be real as well.

SPRING BEE

Aboard the reefer vessel SPRING BEE, a Myanmar seafarer lost his flashlight. A flashlight was an important piece of equipment in his job. He had put in a request for a new one, but it takes time for such things to be processed.

Meanwhile, Christmas Day arrived and the crew gathered in the mess. The captain planned to give out the gifts we put onboard during their Christmas morning gathering. Most seafarers on board were not Christian, but enjoyed receiving the gifts anyway. It is always nice to be remembered by the community on land.

As the crew gathered the seafarer mentioned above complained, again, to the chief officer that he still hadn't received a flashlight. The chief officer, jokingly, told him to pick out a Christmas gift first, to be sure to look over all the boxes, and pick out the one with a flashlight in it. The seafarer was not happy his problem was being joked about.

The seafarer begrudgingly took a box out of the twenty-five on the table and held it as the others chose their boxes.

Once they all had a Christmas gift in hand they unwrapped the boxes. Both he and the chief officer stared in amazement as, there, in his box was a new flashlight and batteries. The seafarer began showing everyone his new flashlight, running from one to the other excitedly. No one else received a flashlight in their box that day. It was unexplainable in terms of logic. The words weren't spoken among them that day, but later, when the ship returned and they recounted the event with me they were describing a Christmas miracle.

WISHING TO REMAIN ANONYMOUS

One day in 1996, I met a Romanian seafarer when I visited his ship. He was very sad. I made sure I took time to visit with him after greeting the others on board. I asked him if he felt like talking. In the midst of our conversation I was not surprised to hear that this man, who looked exhausted, was already on board for over two years! We talked a long time that day and I decided he looked and sounded down enough to be placed on my "intensive" care list. I asked for his ship's address. Immediately I began writing him letters to receive in other ports. In a couple of months I received this reply:

Dear Karen,

Hello! I received your letters and I am happy because you did not forget me. I have already been on board 31 months. After I finish my contract with this company I will give up the seaman's life. I made my mind and decided not to come back to other ship. I do not like this life. It isn't my will. I was forced to go for it. The reason? Money, of course. I earn in one month here the equivalent of ten months in my country. Maybe for other men the money is all, for me it is different. I want to live my life in peace, out of danger, to be together with my family and my friends. All the seamen which make this profession they are not married with their wives, they are married with the sea. They love her, have faith in her, and die for her. I am not like this. What do you think? Am I wrong? I didn't tell to anybody my decision. I wait for your letter.

I wrote this young man back and told him it was ultimately his decision alone to leave the sea or to take a vacation and sign back on. He needed to search his inner self deeply for what it is that he really wanted. He needed to think about what was best for himself and for his family. I knew he was very tired. Working thirty-one months straight on a ship is not only exhausting, it is dangerous. His mind was constantly longing to be home with his family. He was stretching out his time at sea to save money to be able to stay at home a long time. His decision to leave the maritime industry was based mostly on his exhaustion of this very long contract, which had been his choice. I urged him to go home for a long vacation and make his decision after a good rest with his family.

He did this and in the end decided to no longer go back to sea. He wanted to stay with his family. He found a job in the port in his country. The pay, as he said, was only a fraction of what he made on board, but he says it is worth having less but having a life with his wife and children.

JOSE

On a visit to a Cyprus flagged tanker vessel, I found chief cook, Jose, is the galley working hard. Jose took a break to sit down for some coffee and conversation. Jose is a Filipino seafarer. He had been sailing about twenty years. He went to sea to make a better living to support his family. This was Jose's last trip. When he finished this contract in September he was going to retire.

Jose spoke about his life at sea. He echoed the sentiment of many married seafarers. His contracts were long, vacations short. His children grew up without a father. Jose made sure he gave plenty of credit to his wife who did a wonderful job of raising their three children.

When asked if he planned to use his retirement years to get to know his children better, Jose replied, "It's no use." He explained that his children were all married now and have moved away. One daughter and her family had immigrated to Canada. The others are in provinces. He said his chance to be a father was gone. Jose said that seafarers from developing nations like the Philippines are not seafarers because they love the sea. He understand that seafarers from other countries can go to sea on shorter contracts, stay home longer on vacations, and really be a part of their family. In his view, seafarers like himself sacrifice it all so that their families will survive. It was a price they are willing to pay, although they suffer greatly.

Jose said he will go home in September and live on land with his wife. He wondered what it will be like since they, too, did not know each other very well. He was looking forward to relaxing after twenty years of hard work away from his home, but he was nervous with thoughts of how he will fit in.

TWO BROTHERS

The M/V VANCOUVER came into Galveston to load grain over the Fourth of July in 1997. As I visited with the crew, I met Lito, the ship's radio officer. We began talking about his job and his family. He told me his older brother, also a seafarer, helped him get into the profession. Lito's job as a radio officer was in danger because radio officers were becoming obsolete with the dawn of new technology. Lito was concerned about his future. He said his brother, Norberto, was a chief officer.

It had been twelve years since Lito had seen his brother. Their contracts were each for one year, but their vacations fell at different times. The ironic part of this story is that Lito and Noberto live in the same house outside of Manila with their wives and children. Their wives are sisters.

Once, a few years ago, Lito's ship was docking in Matadi, Zaire. As they came closer to the pier, he could see the name of the ship already docked in the berth near theirs. It was his brother's ship. As soon as his ship was cleared he ran down the gangway and over to the other ship. Anxious to finally see his brother, he asked the AB on deck where Norberto was only to be told his brother has signed off earlier that day and was gone.

When I asked Lito the name of his brother's current ship he said, "AFRICAN CAMELIA." That was a ship that we saw in Galveston every once in a while! I told him I would look for

Norberto the next time the AFRICAN CAMELIA came into port.

THE DEL MONTE TRANSPORTER

In December of 1997, just as we had done for many years, we collected Christmas gifts for the seafarers coming into our port. Church and community groups, individuals and families alike brought gifts to the Seafarers Center in November and December and we distributed the gifts aboard ships throughout those weeks leading up to Christmas.

Every week that year, we saw the DEL MONTE TRANSPORTER come in on Fridays. They came from Guatemala bringing bananas to our port. The same crew had been on board since January. We knew them well.

On December 19th, I delivered the Christmas gifts to the Latvian, Lithuanian, and Russian seafarers aboard this ship. They were surprised and childlike with excitement. Never before had they received Christmas gifts on their ship. They came from all over the ship to see the colorful boxes stacked on the table in the lounge. It was a magical beginning of a special holiday.

On many ships when the gifts are delivered, the presents are stored until Christmas Eve or Christmas morning. Then the crew gathers together for a special meal, celebration, and receive their gifts.

The following week the DEL MONTE TRANSPORTER arrived in Galveston the day after Christmas. When I went to visit, Captain Victor told me about their Christmas. He said on Christmas morning at sea, they all gathered on the bridge. They had a moment of silence, and then it was time to open their gifts. They were very anxious to open the gifts but instead of ripping into them, Captain Victor said each man opened his gift carefully, not to tear the paper. They were so overwhelmed by the kindness of the people in our community that they decided to take the gifts home just as they received them to show their families. Most were signing off the next week. They had been on board a year. As Captain Victor relayed the story to me, his eyes teared up and voice grew quiet. He said after the silence of opening the gifts in awe, the seafarers began to sing Christmas songs and wished each other good health. They had a special meal that day and celebrated the special love they felt from people they never met.

CARMELITO

In late February of 1998, aboard a research vessel working in the Gulf of Mexico, a Filipino seafarer named Carmelito suffered a terrible accident. Carmelito fell, striking his head, which caused a skull fracture. He was brought by helicopter to our hospital in Galveston and underwent surgery. He lay in a coma for three weeks.

I began visiting Carmelito when a seafarer from a sister ship docked in Galveston told me about him. Every day I went to the hospital where I prayed at his bedside. The nurses told me patients in comas can hear what is going on around them, so I began talking to him and singing to him. The seafarers from his sister ship visited him while they were in port.

When I first went to the hospital I spoke with the hospital social worker. She gave me his wife's phone number in Manila. I contacted Fr. Savino Bernadi, our Apostleship of the Sea port chaplain in Manila, so that he could visit the family. I also spoke by telephone to Carmelito's wife to let her know he was not alone.

One day while I was visiting Carmelito, he opened his eyes. He still could not speak or respond, eat or breathe on his own. I continued to talk to him and pray with him. I began reading him short stories. When he was interested in the story he'd keep his eyes open. Every day I talked to him about finding his way back.

The shipping company was going to bring his wife to be with him but there was a problem in obtaining a US visa for her. The company decided on hiring an air ambulance service to take Carmelito to a hospital in Manila.

I used my then monthly column in the *Catholic Maritime News*, to tell Carmelito's story and ask for prayers. The newsletter was published in Washington D.C. and went out worldwide. On Holy Thursday, aboard the M/V ALLIGATOR STRENGTH in the port of Oakland, California, port chaplain, Deacon Stanley Lee shared Carmelito's story with the crew. At their communion service that day they decided to collect some money to send to Carmelito's wife to help with expenses.

The company which owned the ship on which Carmelito was injured took very good care of him and his family. Carmelito left Galveston on April 25, 1998 to return home to the Philippines aboard an air ambulance with a doctor on board. He was taken to St. Luke's Hospital in Manila until he was well enough to go home. Carmelito suffered brain damage and has to have constant care from his wife and family. I continue my prayers for them.

BEN'S GIFT

In July 1998 the ALAM ACAPULCO, a bulk ship, called in the port of Galveston. Ben is a Filipino seafarer who worked as the 3rd engineer aboard the ship. When they were here he made a relatively simple request. He asked if he ordered a TV antenna for his home, would it be okay to have it delivered to the Seafarers Center. The ALAM ACULPULCO was on a regular run from Mexico to Galveston so he could pick it up when they got back. "No problem!" I said. He ordered it, it was delivered and when their ship came back to Galveston I delivered it to the ship. He was very grateful.

At the Seafarers Center we help the seafarers out the best we can in simple ways. I didn't think anything more about it until around Christmas that year. The ALAM VERACRUZ came into port. This is a sister ship of the ship Ben was on. I visited the ship and as soon as the seafarers heard my name one of them went running. Soon he returned with a beautiful hand crafted wooden tall ship model that had my name painted on the stern. The young seafarer who handed it to me said, "This is from Ben, the 2nd engineer on the ALAM MEXICO." He explained that Ben was promoted and moved to another vessel that didn't trade in Galveston.

There was also a letter. Opening the letter I read:

Dear Ate Karen,

I am thinking all the time of how I can repay you for your kindness, so I buy this gift for Christmas for you in Mexico. It's an expedition ship model (tall ship-handmade) bearing your name! But I am unlucky because I suppose to hand it to you in person but my port of call is always New Orleans. I have a friend on ALAM VERACRUZ, 4th engineer Manuel, and their ship is coming to Galveston so I ask him to deliver this gift to you. I hope you like it.

Extend my best regards to all personnel at the Center and advance Merry Christmas too!

Ben

That beautiful wooden ship graced my desk for ten years until my office was sadly destroyed in Hurricane Ike.

PINOY

"Ate, Karen! I need your help!" The word, "Ate", pronounced, "At- tee", is a Filipino term for elder sister. On the other end of a long distance phone line a young cadet pleaded for help. He was calling from Athens, Greece.

I met Pinoy when I went to the Philippines in October of 1997 to attend the World Congress of the Apostleship of the Sea. He and several other cadets from the University Cebu had also attended. After the Congress I spent some time in Cebu with the cadets. I told them once they were sailing that if they ever needed help they could go to any port chaplain and ask for help. Pinoy remembered what I said.

Pinoy graduated shortly after the Congress and went to Manila to apply for work with a manning agency. In October 1998 he wrote:

Dear Ate Karen,

Hi! Hello, how are you? Well everything is fine. I miss you, Ate. Until now I'm still here in Manila waiting for my schedule to depart but I don't know my address yet.

Everyday I call my company just to know about my situation. They said that I have a ship maybe by end of this month. I hope so. Anyway, I am praying so hard to have a better life.

I met one of your friends. His name is Alfredo from Iloilo. I greet him- I recognize him because he is wearing the Galveston Seafarers Center t-shirt. As of now that is all my news. Always pray for me.

Your kapatid (brother),
Pinoy

Pinoy was sent by his agency in Manila to his first assignment in Athens, Greece. He was employed there by a Greek yacht owner. He went with eager enthusiasm. He, like so many other young seafarers, is the hope of his family's future. Soon, however, Pinoy came to realize his first experience as a seafarer was not going to be a good one.

The yacht owner was also the captain of the vessel. Pinoy's contract was to be for two years with a guaranteed day off once a week. He was to have 80% of his salary sent home to his parents and receive 20% monthly on board. Instead the owner worked him sixteen hours a day with no days off for three months. His parents hadn't received their allotment and Pinoy was given only a small food allowance.

The owner was hard on him. He verbally abused him calling him degrading names in Greek in front of passengers. He made him pay back food allowance money when he felt Pinoy wasn't working hard enough. There was one other Filipino working on board but after a run-in with the captain he disappeared. Pinoy was alone and scared.

Pinoy

The verbal abuse became worse. Pinoy worked diligently and carefully, trying to please the captain. But no matter how hard he tried, the captain found fault.

Pinoy and I had been corresponding prior to the phone

call. Through his letters he began trusting me with his pain. He wrote:

> I am AB and messman here... two positions. My master is the owner...I ask the Lord for protection....
>
> ....I am staying in the house at night and working on the yacht by day...But before going to the yacht I must do backyard cleaning like cutting grass....there are only two of us on board and we cook our own food....
>
> ....I celebrated Easter in the yacht. I have no time to go out for Eucharist....I stay in the yacht now and work all the time. They are not following the working hours in my contract. I'm very tired all the day and there is no extra pay. In the contract it states I have a day off once a week but in one month I work, still no day off.
>
> ...Every time I do good work I'm given 5000 dracmas. Every time I make mistake I pay $20 US. My employer is not kind. He always shout bad words at me. I keep to myself but I don't know how to survive. My contract is for two years!....I know you are worried about me but I can still handle it.
>
> ...He only gives food allowance and until now I didn't receive my salary. I'm praying that God enlightens this man's mind to understand what is life. Another captain here told me that my master is bad. Every employee who deploy in his yacht never survive. After two or three months disappear. Now they do it to me. I'm hoping that I am the last Filipino. I don't want to send Filipino seamen to this Greek man.
>
> ....Now I have another complaint. I have no food provision on

board. The money for food allowance is not enough. Until now I haven't received my salary. I ask at the office and they say, "Later!"

Pinoy's situation was clearly getting worse. I advised him to call the Philippine Embassy in Piraeus to inform them of his situation.

....*I received your letter. I informed the Philippine Embassy and they are monitoring my situation.*

That letter was written June 1, 1998. It was the last letter I received from Pinoy before his phone call. "Ate Karen, please help me!" I knew Pinoy was pushed to the edge. He had tried so hard to endure. He said he had lost a lot of weight due to lack of food and was exhausted as well. But mostly he was frightened. The captain had threatened to kill him. He was calling at 3:00am Greek time, using what was left of his food allowance money to make the call. He promised to make his way to Piraeus to go to the Philippine Embassy for help the next day.

The next morning at 3:00am Galveston time I called the Philippine Embassy to see if Pinoy made it there. As I was on the phone with a staff member of the Embassy, Pinoy walked in the door. The staff member asked me if I wanted to speak with him. When Pinoy came on the line he said, "Thank you, Ate," and then broke down in relief that is was finally over. Not able to continue speaking he handed the phone back to the Embassy worker. I explained what was going on and Pinoy was granted protection until they could work out his repatriation. Pinoy was at the Embassy for a week as the paperwork was being filled out.

The yacht owner denied any wrongdoing when confronted by Embassy officials. The owner demanded they send Pinoy back to work. They refused saying Pinoy would remain in the protection of the Philippine Embassy until he is returned home to Manila.

Pinoy learned a hard lesson with his first shipboard experience. Now he is more careful in accepting positions and has been working hard and steady for many years. He is now married and has a beautiful family.

RODERICK

As I visited the crew of the M/V RACHEL B, I noticed one young Filipino seafarer off to the side and quiet. Eventually I made my way over to him and asked his name. "Roderick," he said. I asked him if this was his first ship. He was surprised that I knew that. I told him I could tell it was, and he began talking about being homesick. He described the loneliness he felt, especially his first Christmas away from his family…away from everything! They were at sea on Christmas and it was difficult.

I told him about my trip to the Philippines in 1997 and work with the cadets in Cebu. He was smiling when he heard that I wrote to several of the cadets on board ships. He learned the preciousness of letters from home. They are few and far between, but so very much needed. He liked the idea that the Cebu cadets call me "Ate."

I visited Roderick several times on board and he came with

his shipmates to the Seafarers Center too. The RACHEL B was in for repairs so as things began to look like they were going to leave soon, Roderick brought me a gift. It was a little stuffed gorilla. I had never seen anything like it. He said he thought it would make me smile when I was working in my office. I put the little gorilla on my desk to remind me of Roderick.

When Roderick gave me his address to write him I noticed his family name immediately. I had another seafarer on my correspondence list with the same family name. When I opened my address notebook to that seafarer's name I saw that Roderick's home address was on the same street, in the same village. I asked Roderick if he was related to a seafarer named Domingo and he said Domingo was his uncle.

Domingo was in our hospital five years earlier when he was injured aboard his vessel. I visited him in the hospital until he was sent home. What a small world! Before his ship left port, I gave Roderick a letter for the voyage. It was his first letter from his new, "Ate Karen."

A HOMECOMING

The joy felt by seafarers going home is indescribable. In November of 2000 I had the opportunity to travel back to the Philippines to attend a conference in Cebu. I was in the Philippines three years earlier for the Apostleship of the Sea World Congress in Davao. Following that Congress, I travelled to Cebu and spent time with the maritime cadets there. We formed a great bond, and during the three years since that first visit I continued to correspond with them.

Some graduated and went aboard ship and some new cadets came in. So going back to Cebu was my homecoming of sorts.

It was a trip more than attending a conference. It was a deep experience for me. Upon my arrival, the cadets and I came together along with Fr. Roland Doriol, SJ., port chaplain of Cebu. We had a wonderful sharing session and dinner together. Afterwards the cadets and I went up to "Cebu Tops" to overlook the city at twilight. In the dark on the mountain we all sat together and talked about so many things.

The next day we all met again at the Cebu Seafarers Center and were joined by the wives of seafarers from Cebu. Again we had a sharing session. The wives had many questions about their husbands' lives at sea. I was pleased to meet the wives of the seafarers we took care of in Galveston. Again we shared a meal.

I then went to the conference center and began an intense five day seminar on, "Crisis Preparedness." There were lectures and workshops where chaplains from all over Asia and two from U.S. ports participated. It was during that time that the 2000 presidential election was going on in the U.S. I voted early before leaving Texas. The CNN station monitored by different people attending the conference kept us informed on the election returns. Several of the Asian chaplains are U.S. missionaries so many people were interested.

As the reports came in, it was quite interesting to see the reaction of the European missionaries and Asian people. We had missed the call for Al Gore winning the State of Florida, but when it was called again, announcing George Bush as the winner, the whole place groaned and gave us condolences. Then, as the uncertainty was reported, they began to raise their hopes. As a U.S. citizen watching this from the outside of our country, I found it extremely interesting.

The political structure within the Philippines was very shaky. Their president in 2000 was Joseph Estrada and he was being tried for impeachment while I was there. There were national days of prayer where millions gathered in the streets to pray for their country. A general strike was called and workers took to the streets to protest. It was an uneasy time.

Following the conference, I left Cebu and travelled to Davao for the dedication of our new Stella Maris (Star of the Sea) Seafarers Center there. It was a beautiful new center and the dedication went well. While in Davao I spent time with the Stella Maris staff and met the wives of the seafarers from Davao.

On the very last day in this beautiful country, I flew to Manila to change planes for the States. In Manila I had several hours before my flight. At the airport I was met by Eduardo, a seafarer I had not seen in ten years! We met in October 1990 when I was in New York studying seafarers rights at the Center for Seafarers Rights. We helped him there and we have corresponded ever since.

Eduardo just finished his ship's contract and came home. I was just leaving. We had three hours together in which I met his family and had a great visit. Then, when he took me back to the airport to catch my flight another seafarer, Orly, and his wife came to see me. Orly is one of the "CYCLONE" crew (Unconditional Love Story: Meeting the People of the Sea, Mall Publishing 1997). It was great to see them too! It was a great trip.

Tired and ready to go home, I got in line for check in. There, in front of me were fifteen Filipino men standing together to check in as well. I smiled....seafarers. I introduced myself and so it began. We travelled together from Manila to San Francisco to Atlanta and then changed planes again in Atlanta. The travel time was about nineteen hours. We parted in Atlanta. They were going to join their ship in Charleston, South Carolina. I flew to Houston. It was very appropriate that my trip would end the way it began, with seafarers.

MIKOLA

In April 2001, Mikola, a Ukrainian seafarer, fell approximately six meters and was seriously injured aboard his ship in the Gulf of Mexico. The U.S. Coast Guard air lifted him to the hospital in Galveston. The next day I was reading our local newspaper and saw a small article about the accident. I went to the hospital to visit him. His injuries included two broken arms, several broken bones in his face, and many bruises and scrapes.

Mikola was told he would have surgery in two days. On the morning of the surgery I went to the hospital and found the surgery was postponed until Monday. That was not a good sign when dealing with shipping companies. Sometimes the companies want the seafarer transferred to a hospital in his home country where the medical costs are less. I spoke with the nurses and found no one from the company had even contacted the hospital following Mikola's arrival there.

In cases of seafarers' illness or injury the shipping company they work for is responsible for his/her medical care. No one had heard from the company. Mikola's family had not been notified.

Mikola and I communicated well with each other– he, with his broken English, and me, with my very broken Russian. Twice I made him laugh when I mispronounced a word. As you might well imagine, laughing with broken face bones is painful.

Mikola told me his wife's name is Tamara and that she is a journalist at the *Odessa Evening* newspaper. He said he was the youngest of ten children. Five of his brothers were killed in WWII as they fought the Germans. A sixth sibling died of hunger in 1947. Now there were just four of them. Mikola and Tamara have two sons, both seafarers.

I contacted the British and International Seafarer Society's chaplain in Odessa and gave him the information about Mikola and his family. The chaplain there was able to find Tamara at the *Odessa Evening* newspaper and gave her my email address. She contacted me and I began sending her daily reports on Mikola's condition.

On the day Mikola had surgery, I arrived early just as they were wheeling him down. I met him in the hallway. As I was giving him a blessing, the hospital social worker ran up to ask him, again, who was going to pay his hospital bill. Still no one from the company or even a shipping agent called to set up the billing. Mikola was worried the surgery would be cancelled again. I spoke with the social worker and promised to find a phone number for the ship agent and the name of the company for her.

While Mikola was in surgery I worked the phones locating the ship agent handling his ship, which had just docked in Houston. I gave the information to the social worker.

Mikola spent the next full day in the surgical intensive care unit. He had his arm bones set and there were rods in screws coming out of both arms. He also had metal plates put in his face, above and below his right eye and upper right jaw. He lost three teeth and the others were extremely sore.

I was visiting twice a day. We had good conversations. I kept Tamara informed via email and when Mikoka was feeling well enough I helped him call home. He couldn't hold the phone so I held it for him. His son, Andrej, just got home from his ship's contract so Mikola was able to speak with him and Tamara. They were so relieved to hear his voice and he felt so much better talking to them.

While he was in the hospital, Mikola celebrated his 50th birthday. The students in the theology class I was teaching that year made him a large wall poster wishing him a happy birthday and all the students signed it. They were praying for him daily since his accident.

Less than a week after his surgery, rumors were surfacing about him being sent home. He told me he was worried and asked me to help delay it if possible. He was afraid the cabin pressure on the plane would harm him, especially his facial injuries. His sinuses were still draining blood.

I spoke to the social worker who assured me he would be safe. I insisted on talking with his doctors. The doctors said there was no reason to keep him any longer. The company was pressuring him to go home. Mikola resigned himself to leaving and asked me only to call his home in three days to see if he made it okay.

Mikola left for home with a travel itinerary that had him flying from Houston to Chicago to Frankfurt to Kiev. He would not be accompanied. Without the use of his arms and unable to eat solid foods, the trip promised to be grueling to say the least. His two major concerns were how would he eat and how would he be able to use the toilet on the plane?

The aids had laid out his clothing, including a pair of zippered pants and a belt. No one was thinking that these pants would be difficult for him to remove if necessary. I ran to the store and bought him a pair of elastic waist sweat pants for the trip. When I came in with the elastic waist pants, he nearly cried.

Mikola left for the airport that day. And as promised, in three days I called his home. Tamara answered the phone and said that he made it home. He was exhausted but happy to be there with them. She thanked me for looking after him while he was here with us.

VICTOR

Sometimes they are lonely. Victor is a chief engineer from Latvia. He came to the Seafarers Center during his lunch hour break. He didn't have any business to take care of such as a phone call home or shopping. He just wanted to be with people. When his time was up, he said good-bye and invited me to visit aboard his ship. Something told me he needed company.

I went to Victor's ship that afternoon at coffee time. When Victor heard I was on board, he came down from his office. He showed me into the Officers' Mess and began to play host bringing out cookies, making tea and sandwiches. He was talking about his family at home and entertaining guests at his house whenever he is there. He asked many times if I would like more tea or another sandwich. He was clearly having fun. Other officers were smiling watching him serve them as well. The chief officer said, "He likes when we have visitors." That was very evident.

When it was time to leave, Victor was sad. He was truly grateful for the time he was able to entertain a guest on board.

YURIJ

In early February of 2006, some familiar faces came back into port. The Russian vessel, AKADEMIK SHATSKIYY, arrived. They came into Galveston every few months, but spent most of their time in the Gulf of Mexico doing research.

The year before, I got to know the 2nd officer, Andrea. He came to the Seafarers Center and I also visited with him on board. He was having some problems and it helped to talk them out. This day when I boarded the ship, Andrea came out to greet me and told me his chief officer, Yurij, just received news his father died. The company said he could not go home for his funeral and Andrea said that Yurij was in bad shape. Andrea asked if I would come back at noon and pick them both up. He wanted to take Yurij ashore to get him away from the ship for a while.

At noon I returned and Andrea and Yurij went ashore. When I dropped them off I asked Yurij if he wanted me to visit him the next day to talk. He said yes.

The next day I went to the ship and Yurij came out on the deck. We had a long talk. Yurij lost his wife five years previously and his mother two years after that. Losing his father was too much for him. He begged to go home but the ship could not be left without a chief officer. The company said it was impossible to get a replacement on such short notice. Yurij grieved. His shipmates felt his pain and felt helpless to relieve it.

Every day I went to the ship and met him on the deck to listen as he talked. Mostly he spoke about how hard a life it is to work on the sea, to be away from home so long, to be separated from family when they needed him the most. He felt deeply alone and spoke as if I wasn't there, yet he knew someone was listening.

The AKADEMIK SHATSKIYY left port a few days later. I gave Yurij a letter to read on his voyage. The ship returned the end of March. As I walked down the pier, Yurij ran down the gangway to greet me. He smiled and said, "Next month I go home!" We stood on the pier and talked a while. He said he is working through his grief. He looked so much better than weeks earlier. It was great to see him again.

Padre Sergio handed me the last piece of pear. I was rested; I was no longer hungry or thirsty. I was given food for my body and food for my soul. Lifelong lessons to nurture within myself and share with others; Respect, Dignity, Love, Peace, Serenity, and Humility.

About the Author

Karen Parsons OFS is a Catholic Ecclesial Lay Minister serving as an Apostleship of the Sea chaplain in the ports of Galveston and Texas City, Texas. She began her port ministry career over 29 years ago in the port of Detroit, Michigan.

Karen is a graduate of and has been on the faculty of the Houston Port Chaplaincy School since 1990. She has also conducted seminars and workshops in South Africa, Australia, and Brazil and has travelled to every continent except Antarctica for training in this field.

She received her certification in Spiritual Direction through the Spiritual Direction Institute in Houston in 2007.

About the Publisher

The North American Maritime Ministry Association, NAMMA, a Christian association, provides fellowship, encouragement, advocacy, education and spiritual and professional development for those in maritime ministry. Visit us at www.namma.org.